four
for lunch
...dinner
for eight

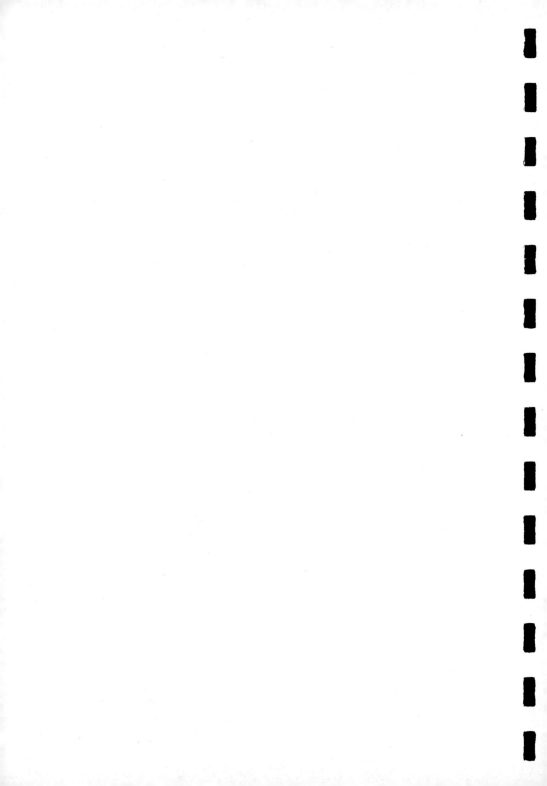

four
for lunch
...dinner
for eight

ZOË SHIPPEN

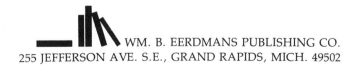

WM. B. EERDMANS PUBLISHING CO.
255 JEFFERSON AVE. S.E., GRAND RAPIDS, MICH. 49502

Library of Congress Cataloging in Publication Data

Shippen, Zoë.
    Four for lunch, dinner for eight.
        1. Luncheons.   2. Dinners and dining.
3. Cookery. I. Title.
TX735.S48   641.5'3   75-14073
ISBN 0-8028-3462-0

This book is dedicated first of all to my wonderful husband, whose interest and cooperation in all that I undertake have been most helpful. Then to all the kind friends who have been amiable "guinea pigs," tasting my many concoctions.

I would like to thank my sweet secretary, Cathy Smith (Mrs. David R. Smith), who helped type the manuscript of this cookbook, and also Ms. Martha Bentley, for her charming illustrations.

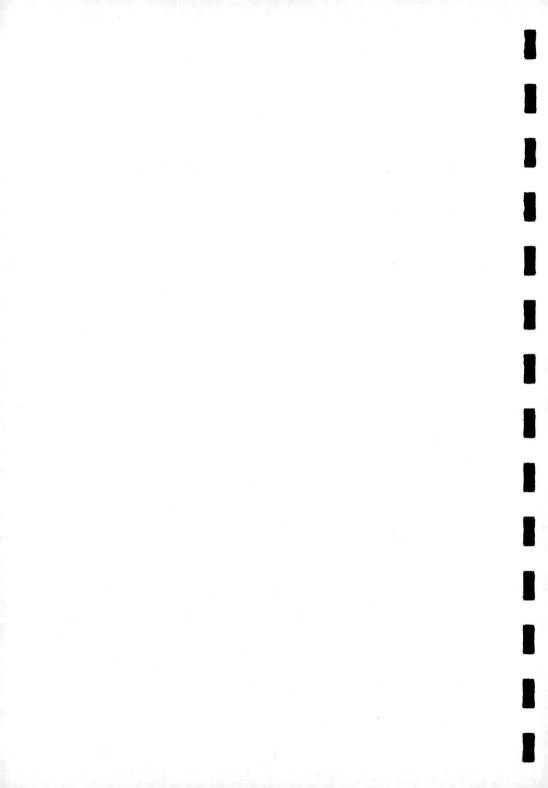

contents

introduction

Meal planning for entertaining always requires much thought, and luncheons are especially difficult. You want to make your menus interesting, well balanced, with enough to eat, but not too much. Dinners are usually planned so that you can fix things ahead of time, leaving more time to spend with your guests. But in all your company menus you want something a little unusual so that you will be considered a gourmet hostess, not an unimaginative one. Since help is often impossible to get, you naturally want quick and easy recipes.

The first part of this book deals with complete luncheon menus, and the second part with dinners—simple enough for every day but delicious enough for company entertaining. The third part of the book itemizes recipes for the supplementary dishes mentioned in the luncheon and dinner menus, as well as providing other new and interesting recipes for your own planning. Your guests will be intrigued by many of the unusual and original recipes in this book, especially the soups, chicken dishes, and desserts.

SERVING SUGGESTIONS

When eight or more people have to be served without a maid's help, buffet style is necessary. While guests serve themselves, the food may be kept warm on a hot tray plus a chafing dish or electrical skillet. If you want to serve soup at your buffet dinner, I would advise passing it in bouillon cups in the living room. This will eliminate guests leaving the table once they are seated. When dessert time comes, I bring the dessert to the tables—again no confusion of guests getting up.

BREADS

Fancy breads or rolls are welcome at lunch, but we never serve bread at dinner in our house. If your guests are not weight-watchers, you may include hot buttered rolls. And crackers are almost necessary with soup. Those refrigerated rolls and biscuits are so quick to fix that I highly recommend them. The crescent rolls are extremely adaptable for various fillings—and can be cut in half to make "mini buns," especially for ladies' luncheons. (See directions under pages for breads.)

BEVERAGES

For lunch most people like tea—hot or iced. Have a kettle of hot water ready on the stove, with cups nearby, and a bucket of ice ready to pop in glasses. (Those iced tea mixes are marvelous.) After dinner we serve Sanka in demitasses to everyone, with no questions asked. If someone *should* ask for real coffee, one can quickly fix it with the instant variety.

DESSERTS

You will notice that most of these are fruit desserts —especially to please the weight-watchers. If some of your guests are *not*, they can indulge in the cookies while the dieters can forgo them. The nice part about desserts is that they can be made ahead of time—the frozen ones even weeks ahead. People usually expect some sort of sweet finish to a meal, and it will leave a pleasant lasting impression. These dessert recipes were made to serve four for luncheons: don't forget to double them to serve eight for dinner parties.

—Zoë Shippen

part I

luncheons for four

**hot seafood
hot chicken
hot egg
hot meat
seafood salad
chicken salad**

MENU

BAKED CRAB AND CHICKEN SANDWICH
Fruit and Vegetable Salad
Rum Chiffon
Candy Cookie Bars

*   *   *

COMMENTS: A rather unusual but especially delicious entree. Since you get both vegetables and fruit in the salad you can have a nonfruity dessert. Very few calories in the dessert, though it *feels* creamy. However, you'll make up for that with those yummy cookie bars!

BAKED CRAB AND CHICKEN SANDWICH

4 thick slices bread	½ cup crab meat
4 teaspoons soft butter	½ cup diced cooked chicken
1 egg, beaten	½ cup cream of mushroom
½ cup milk	soup (undiluted)
2 teaspoons margarine	¼ cup dairy sour cream
¼ cup chopped onion	⅓ cup cream sherry

Trim bread to neat squares and spread with butter (or soft margarine). Put in 4 individual shallow, greased baking dishes, butter side down. Beat egg, add milk; pour over bread. Melt margarine and sauté onion until tender. Add remaining ingredients; spoon over bread. Bake at 350° for 20-25 minutes. Serve garnished with watercress or chopped chives. (Serves 4)

IN ADVANCE: Make your cookies the day before—also the salad dressing. If you have no diced chicken on hand, cook a chicken for it. First thing the morning of your party make the dessert—the longer it chills the better it tastes.

THE OTHER RECIPES: Fruit and vegetable salad (page 101); rum chiffon (page 135); candy cookie bars (page 143).

SUBSTITUTIONS: This is so well balanced I wouldn't advise any substitutions, except for the dessert and cookies. You could have a fancy ice cream and less fattening cookies, such as coffee cookies.

MENU

SCALLOPS IN COCKLE SHELLS
Bacon Cheese Mini Buns
Tomato Artichoke Aspic
Nectarine Sherbet
Macaroon Crumb Cookies

* * *

COMMENTS: A real "company" menu, yet not rich (unless people overindulge in those bacon cheese buns). The nectarine sherbet is sensational with its almond flavor, teamed with chewy almond cookies.

SCALLOPS IN COCKLE SHELLS

½ clove garlic, minced
2 tablespoons butter
12 scallops, cut in fourths
¼ lb. fresh mushrooms, sliced
1 tablespoon flour

½ teaspoon onion salt
Dash ground pepper
½ cup milk
3 tablespoons Madeira
¼ cup toasted almonds

Sauté garlic in butter with scallops and mushrooms for 3 minutes. Remove ingredients and transfer to a bowl. Without washing skillet add flour and seasonings, then milk gradually. Cook, stirring, until thick. Add scallop mixture and wine. Divide into 4 baking shells and bake at 350° for 30 minutes. Serve sprinkled with toasted almonds. Garnish with parsley, if desired. (Serves 4)

IN ADVANCE: You can make the molded salad, the frozen dessert, and the cookies a day in advance, leaving you plenty of time on your party morning.

THE OTHER RECIPES: Mini buns (page 93); tomato artichoke aspic (page 107); nectarine sherbet (page 118); macaroon crumb cookies (page 142).

SUBSTITUTIONS: Sesame mini buns for the bacon cheese mini buns; any other molded vegetable salad; any fruit dessert (not molded).

MENU

TUNA GRANADA
Cheese Biscuits
Bottled Kumquats
Apricot Carrot Salad Mold
Anise Crumb Cookies

* * *

COMMENTS: This entree is quick, easy, and tasty. It can be served in individual baking dishes, if you like. The salad in this case doubles as a dessert. One very seldom sees anise cookies, so they will be a treat—chewy and crunchy.

TUNA GRANADA

1 can (7 oz.) albacore tuna
2 tablespoons spaghetti
    sauce mix
1 tablespoon instant onion
8 sliced, stuffed olives

½ cup milk
¼ cup tomato paste
1 cup condensed cream of
    chicken soup

Flake tuna with a fork. Add remaining ingredients and mix well. Cook about 5 minutes. (Serves 4)

IN ADVANCE: You can make the molded salad and the cookies ahead of time.

THE OTHER RECIPES: Cheese biscuits (page 88); apricot carrot salad mold (page 112); anise crumb cookies (page 143).

SUBSTITUTIONS: Fruit avocado dessert salad for the apricot carrot salad mold; any other cookies.

MENU

CHICKEN OLIVE CASSEROLE
Mini Buns
Golden Fruit Salad
Blissful Dream Ice Cream
Chewy Bread Crumb Macaroons

* * *

COMMENTS: This casserole is very tasty and quick to fix. If you want to make an "extra-special" luncheon, put 2 or 3 spears of cooked asparagus on each plate beside a serving of the chicken, then pour the sauce over both. The salad is refreshing, and the dessert speaks for itself.

CHICKEN OLIVE CASSEROLE

¾ cup cooked rice
2 tablespoons melted
    margarine
1½ cups cooked chicken
½ cup diced celery
3 tablespoons minced
    pimiento

½ cup diced stuffed olives
⅔ cup cream of celery soup
1 egg, beaten well
CHICKEN HOLLANDAISE
    SAUCE

Combine rice and melted margarine; add remaining ingredients except beaten egg. Mix well, then fold in egg. Bake in greased casserole at 350° about 30 minutes. Serve with CHICKEN HOL-LANDAISE SAUCE. (Serves 4)

CHICKEN HOLLANDAISE SAUCE

½ cup canned chicken
   gravy
¼ cup dairy sour cream

2 tablespoons margarine
2 tablespoons lemon juice
1 egg yolk

In small saucepan mix gravy and sour cream; heat, but do not boil. In another small saucepan melt margarine; add lemon juice and egg yolk. Stir over low heat until it starts to thicken, then stir in soup mixture. Heat, but do not allow to boil. (Serves 4)

IN ADVANCE: The molded salad, ice cream, and cookies can all be made the day before. Cook a chicken and dice it, if you have no cooked chicken ready.

THE OTHER RECIPES: Mini buns (page 93); golden fruit salad (page 109); blissful dream ice cream (page 123); chewy bread crumb macaroons (page 142).

SUBSTITUTIONS: Any other fruit salad; any other dessert and cookies.

MENU

CHICKEN MUSHROOM CRÊPES
Mixed Vegetable Salad
Crackers
Grape Juice Pear Mold
Pecan Crispies

* * *

COMMENTS: This entree is a luncheon favorite at Kent Country Club in Grand Rapids, Michigan. Their marvelous pastry cook, Irene Wilson, gave me her recipe for the crêpes—the best I have ever tasted. Since the crêpes are starchy, you need no bread; however, crackers might be welcome to nibble with the salad.

CHICKEN MUSHROOM CRÊPES

CRÊPES BATTER:

¼ cup flour
½ teaspoon baking powder
¼ teaspoon salt
½ teaspoon sugar

½ cup milk
1 tablespoon butter
1 egg, well beaten

Sift together dry ingredients; beat egg. Heat milk till warm and add butter, stirring until melted. Remove from heat; add beaten egg and dry ingredients. Beat with rotary beater until smooth. Heat a 5 or 6-inch skillet; grease with Crisco or salad oil. Pour in just enough batter to make a thin coating, tilting to spread evenly. Cook over moderate heat, first on one side, then on the other until browned. Remove each crêpe as made to cookie sheet. Keep warm until ready to fill. (Makes 8-10 crêpes)

CHICKEN MUSHROOM FILLING

2 tablespoons butter
2 tablespoons flour
⅓ cup chicken broth
⅓ cup milk
1 egg yolk (optional)
1¼ cups diced cooked
  chicken

1 jar (2½ oz.) sliced
  mushrooms
3 tablespoons dairy sour
  cream
¼ teaspoon onion salt
  (or more)
2 tablespoons sherry

Melt butter and add flour; cook and stir a few moments. Slowly stir in broth and milk, and cook until thick; add chicken and mushrooms. Keep over very low heat until ready to serve, then mix in egg yolk, sour cream, salt, and sherry until smooth. Heat, but do not boil. Place a big spoonful on lower third of each crêpe and roll into cylinders. Serve warm, 2 for each person. Pass a bowl of mushroom sauce to pour over.

MUSHROOM SAUCE

1 cup condensed cream of
  mushroom soup

½ cup milk

Heat to boiling point.

IN ADVANCE: Have cooked chicken ready. Make your molded dessert and cookies the day before; also the crêpes batter, if you wish, and refrigerate in covered container

THE OTHER RECIPES:
Mixed vegetable salad (page 103); grape juice pear mold (page 129); pecan crispies (page 139).

MENU

Strawberry Borsch
CHEESE ONION QUICHE
Green and White Fruit Salad
Coconut Almond Ice Cream
Almond Crumb Cookies

* * *

COMMENTS: The favorite luncheon dish of many gourmets is "quiche Lorraine," so no luncheon cookbook would be complete without a quiche recipe. We Americans have countless variations of this French specialty, and it has even turned up at cocktail parties in the form of canapes. I hope you will like my onion version.

CHEESE ONION QUICHE

Pre-baked 9" pastry
  shell
2 tablespoons butter
2 cups thinly sliced onions
1 teaspoon seasoned salt
1 teaspoon paprika

½ cup grated Swiss (or
  Gruyere) cheese
4 eggs
1 cup milk
½ cup dairy sour
  cream

Melt butter and sauté onions till almost golden, then cover tightly and let them steam over medium-low heat about 10 minutes. Drain onions and arrange in cooled, baked pastry shell. Sprinkle with salt and paprika, then with grated cheese. Beat eggs, milk, and sour cream together just enough to blend; pour over onions. Bake in preheated 350° oven about 40 minutes until custard is firm. Let stand a few minutes before cutting in wedges. (Serves 8)

CREAM CHEESE PASTRY

½ cup margarine
4 oz. cream cheese

1 cup flour
⅛ teaspoon salt

Mix margarine and cream cheese with wooden spoon; add flour and salt, and mix well. Roll out between 2 sheets of waxed paper and chill in freezer until stiff enough to handle. Fit into 9" pie plate (or layer cake pan), crimp edges, and bake in hot oven until slightly browned.

IN ADVANCE: You can make the cold soup, the ice cream, and cookies the day before. Also, make and refrigerate the pie crust.

THE OTHER RECIPES: Strawberry borsch (page 80); green and white fruit salad (page 108); coconut almond ice cream (page 124); almond crumb cookies (page 142).

SUBSTITUTIONS: Any other fruit salad; any other ice cream.

MENU

DEVILED EGGS BENEDICT
Banana Blueberry Muffins
Green and White Fruit Salad

* * *

COMMENTS: This looks like a skimpy menu but actually is not, because the entree with asparagus and hollandaise sauce is practically a whole meal. Serve muffins with the salad. Since they are sweet, they take the place of a dessert.

DEVILED EGGS BENEDICT

4 slices bread	8 fresh cooked asparagus
1 tablespoon butter	spears
1 can (4½ oz.) deviled ham	1½ cups hollandaise
4 poached eggs	sauce

Toast bread, spread with butter, then with deviled ham. Put a poached egg on top of each slice, arrange asparagus on 1 side, and cover all with the hollandaise. Serve immediately. (Serves 4)

IN ADVANCE: Nothing much you can do the day before, except make the salad dressing. Also, you can bake the muffins, if you like, to reheat just before lunchtime.

THE OTHER RECIPES: Banana blueberry muffins (page 90); green and white fruit salad (page 108).

SUBSTITUTIONS: Best banana bread for the muffins; frozen fruit salad for the salad.

15

MENU

Avocado Green Soup
SPANISH SOUFFLÉ
Corn Muffins
Early October Fruit Salad
Coffee Crunch Ice Cream

*   *   *

COMMENTS: The cold green soup is a nice contrast to the hot soufflé—also an easy way to get your vegetables. Since the ice cream has cookies in it, you don't need any more cookies with this menu.

SPANISH SOUFFLÉ

3 tablespoons margarine
2 tablespoons flour
2 tablespoons tomato paste
½ cup milk
⅓ cup Chef Boyardee
  spaghetti sauce mix with
  tomato base and cheese

½ teaspoon dry mustard
½ teaspoon garlic powder
¼ cup water
¾ cup grated sharp
  Cheddar cheese
3 eggs, separated
12 pimiento-stuffed
  olives, cut-up

Melt margarine, stir in flour, then tomato paste. Gradually add milk. Combine spaghetti sauce mix, mustard, garlic powder, and water; add to first mixture. Cook until thick, then add cheese, stirring until it melts. Cool slightly, then add beaten egg yolks and olives. Fold in stiffly beaten egg whites. Bake in a 1½-quart unbuttered soufflé dish (or 4 individual soufflé dishes) at 375° about 20 minutes for the small dishes and longer for the larger soufflé dish. Serve at once. (Serves 4)

IN ADVANCE: Make the ice cream a day (or days) ahead. You could also make the corn muffins (from a mix or your favorite recipe) and reheat in time to serve with the salad. The soup is a quickie, but be sure to allow plenty of chilling time.

THE OTHER RECIPES: Avocado green soup (page 86); early October fruit salad (page 108); coffee crunch ice cream (page 121).

SUBSTITUTIONS: Any other cold soup; any other fruit salad; any other dessert.

MENU

CHIPPED BEEF TAMAARAA
Toast
Tropical Fruit Salad
Banana Bread

* * *

COMMENTS: "Fabulous!" is what my husband calls this entree. It was inspired by a native feast—called a "Tamaaraa"—we enjoyed in Tahiti, where food liberally laced with coconut milk tasted smoky from the open fire pit. This entree, plus toast, is a balanced meal in itself, very suitably ended with tropical sweets.

CHIPPED BEEF TAMAARAA

½ package frozen chopped spinach
2 tablespoons margarine
2 tablespoons flour
1 cup milk
2 packages (3 oz. each) dried sliced beef

3 tablespoons unsweetened coconut meal *
¼ teaspoon hickory smoked salt
3 tablespoons dairy sour cream
Thin-sliced toast

*available at health food stores

Cook spinach in small amount of water and drain. Cut beef into small pieces with scissors, then rinse with boiling water in a strainer. Melt margarine, add flour, then milk gradually; cook about 3 minutes. Add beef and spinach. Combine coconut meal, smoked salt, and sour cream. Stir into beef mixture just before serving. Serve over thin-sliced toast. (Serves 4)

IN ADVANCE: Make your banana bread or muffins the day before. If muffins, they can be either heated or toasted just before serving. Thaw your spinach first thing in the morning, then make your salad dressing and fix salad greens.

THE OTHER RECIPES: Tropical fruit salad (page 111); banana bread (page 87).

SUBSTITUTIONS: For the salad—any other fruit salad. For the bread—strawberry banana nut bread or banana blueberry muffins.

MENU

Tomato Rhubarb Soup
CHICKEN LIVERS AND MUSHROOMS
Orange Grapefruit Salad
Royal Purple Ice Cream
Almond Crumb Cookies

* * *

COMMENTS: In this menu you drink your vegetables. Quite an interesting soup—the rhubarb adds a refreshing sourness, like lemon. Since the entree is served on toast, you need no buns or muffins. The purple ice cream will evoke compliments.

CHICKEN LIVERS AND MUSHROOMS

½ lb. chicken livers
2 tablespoons margarine
¼ cup chopped onion
½ lb. fresh
  mushrooms
1 teaspoon flour

Dash ground pepper
1 teaspoon soy sauce
¼ cup dairy sour cream
¼ cup cream sherry
Toast points

Cut livers in half. Brown in the margarine, then remove and keep warm. Sauté onion and mushrooms in the same skillet until onion is golden. Stir in flour, pepper, soy sauce, sour cream, and sherry; simmer briefly. Add livers and heat the mixture. Serve on toast points. (Serves 4)

IN ADVANCE: You can make your ice cream and cookies a day or more ahead. Early on the morning of your party, make the salad dressing and fix most of the salad ingredients.

THE OTHER RECIPES: To-mato rhubarb soup (page 78); orange grapefruit salad (page 110); royal purple ice cream (page 122); almond crumb cookies (page 142).

SUBSTITUTIONS: Any other fruit salad or ice cream —perhaps blueberry grape sherry ice cream.

MENU

PIZZA BURGERS
Italian Green Bean Salad
Biscuits
Raspberry Sherry Mousse
Candy Cookie Bars

* * *

COMMENTS: Sounds like rather a plebeian menu, but everyone will like it. The cheesy burgers are very tasty, the salad quite gourmet, with artichoke hearts and those "high class" beans. The dessert and cookies will make a big hit.

PIZZA BURGERS

½ cup finely chopped onion   Dash ground pepper
2 teaspoons margarine   1 lb. ground chuck
⅓ cup tomato paste   ¼ cup tiny cheese cubes
½ teaspoon pizza seasoning   (sharp Cheddar)
½ teaspoon oregano   1 can tomato sauce
¼ teaspoon garlic salt   4 slices toast

Sauté onion in the margarine until almost golden; stir in tomato paste and seasonings, then beef. Lastly, fold in cheese cubes. Form into 4 patties, broil to medium rare, turning once. Serve on toast with tomato sauce. (Serves 4)

IN ADVANCE: You *must* make the bean salad the day before; also the dessert, in order for it to freeze properly and let the sherry "ripen." Cookies can also be made a day or 2 in advance.

THE OTHER RECIPES: Italian green bean salad (page 99); raspberry sherry mousse (page 121); candy cookie bars (page 143).

SUBSTITUTIONS: A molded vegetable salad, such as molded spinach salad or asparagus artichoke mold instead of the bean salad. Another fruit dessert such as ginger fruit cup, or green and white refresher.

23

MENU

Avocado Banana Soup
CURRIED SHRIMP SALAD
Crescent Rolls
Grape Pear Sherbet

* * *

COMMENTS: This is rather a fruity menu, with fruit even in the soup. (Who ever heard of putting banana in soup! But you'll love it.) Curry needs sweet accompaniments, but just so you won't have too many sweet things, we are omitting cookies.

CURRIED SHRIMP SALAD

½ cup mayonnaise
¼ cup dairy sour cream
1 hard-cooked egg yolk, mashed
1 tablespoon lemon juice
1 teaspoon curry powder

1 can (4½ oz.) shrimp
¼ cup diced celery
¾ cup pineapple chunks packed in unsweetened juice, cut in halves
Lettuce

Combine first 5 ingredients; mix well, then add shrimp, celery, and pineapple chunks. Serve on lettuce. (Serves 4)

IN ADVANCE: Make your sherbet the day before. The morning of your party, fix salad ingredients and chill at least 2 hours before lunch time. Fix rolls and refrigerate.

THE OTHER RECIPES: Avocado banana soup (page 83); grape pear sherbet (page 122).

SUBSTITUTIONS: Banana pea soup or curaçao beet soup for the avocado banana soup; frozen pear helene for the grape pear sherbet.

MENU

Consommé Sangria
LOBSTER CHICKEN SALAD
Sesame Mini Buns
Rhubarb Almond Mousse
Chocolate Coconut Cookies

*   *   *

COMMENTS: Your guests will be intrigued by the soup, spiked with Spanish fruited wine, and the unusual dessert (another of my crazy concoctions). The salad is pretty, with touches of red, pale green, and the thick white dressing all through. Since lobster is so expensive, we added chicken to stretch it, and touches of red pimiento to give the illusion of more lobster.

LOBSTER CHICKEN SALAD

½ cup Hellman's
  mayonnaise
¼ cup dairy sour cream
2 tablespoons lemon juice
½ teaspoon seasoned salt
1 teaspoon paprika

1 can (5 oz.) lobster
1 cup diced cooked chicken
2 tablespoons pimiento strips
12 seedless grapes, halved
½ cup diced celery
Lettuce and watercress

Combine first 5 ingredients. Add next 5 ingredients, and mix well. Chill several hours. Serve with lettuce and watercress. (If small grapes are used, do not cut them.) (Serves 4)

IN ADVANCE: Make the mousse and cookies the day before. Have diced chicken ready. First thing on the morning of your luncheon, combine salad ingredients and chill. Wash and chill salad greens. Fix buns and refrigerate in pans till baking time.

THE OTHER RECIPES: Consommé Sangria (page 86); mini buns (page 93); rhubarb almond mousse (page 127), chocolate coconut cookies (page 137).

SUBSTITUTIONS: Mushroom broth for Consommé Sangria; any other fruit dessert; chewy cinnamon cookies for the chocolate coconut cookies.

MENU

Spinach Broth
SALMON RED CAVIAR MOLD
Onion Mini Buns
Pineapple Wine Fruit Cup
Best Ever Lemon Cookies

*   *   *

COMMENTS: This is a colorful salad, decorated with the red caviar. The onion buns are tasty too—just right to go with it. A refreshing fruit cup is the perfect finale.

SALMON RED CAVIAR MOLD

1 envelope plain gelatin
½ cup canned chicken
   broth
¼ cup lemon juice
2 drops red food color
1 hard-boiled egg yolk
¼ cup dairy sour cream
¼ cup cottage cheese

1 can (7¾ oz.) red salmon
2 tablespoons chopped
   pimiento
¼ cup diced celery
1 teaspoon grated onion
¼ cup dairy sour cream
4 teaspoons red caviar
Salad greens

Soften gelatin in the broth 5 minutes. Stir over low heat to dissolve; add lemon juice and red color. In saucer mash egg yolk with a fork; mix in ¼ cup sour cream and the cottage cheese. Stir into gelatin mixture. Remove skin from salmon and break up with a fork; add to gelatin mixture, including liquid from can. Stir in pimiento, celery, and grated onion. Divide equally into 4 individual oiled molds. Chill several hours or overnight. To serve: Unmold on salad plates and surround with lettuce and watercress dribbled with French dressing. Add 1 or 2 cherry tomatoes cut in half to each serving. Put a large spoonful of sour cream on each mold and top with a dab of red caviar. (Serves 4)

IN ADVANCE: Make the salmon mold the day before, also the cookies. The dessert should be made first thing on the morning of your luncheon, so the fruit can be soaking up the wine. Thaw spinach for the soup. Fix your buns and refrigerate in their muffin pans—all ready for baking a few minutes before lunch time.

THE OTHER RECIPES: Spinach broth (page 81); mini buns (page 93); pineapple wine fruit cup (page 132); best ever lemon cookies (page 141).

SUBSTITUTIONS: Tomato cranberry broth for the spinach broth; olive mini buns for the onion buns; ginger fruit cup for pineapple wine fruit cup.

MENU

Tahitian Onion Soup
TUNA MOUSSE
Cheese Biscuits
Tipsy Pears and Raspberries
Chocolate Nut Bars

* * *

COMMENTS: The soup is wild! Don't tell your guests what is in it until they guess (I'm sure they'll like it anyway). Chill your tuna mousse in a large fish mold if you have one and have fun decorating it. The dessert is heavenly—a delightful ending to an interesting meal.

TUNA MOUSSE

1 envelope gelatin
2 tablespoons lemon juice
½ cup boiling chicken broth
½ cup Hellman's mayonnaise
¼ cup yogurt
1 tablespoon minced green
  onion
½ teaspoon dry mustard
1 teaspoon dried dill
  weed
¼ teaspoon pepper
1 can (7 oz.) albacore
  tuna, drained

Soften gelatin in lemon juice in large mixing bowl. Add broth and stir until dissolved. Add remaining ingredients, except tuna; beat until well mixed. Chill 30 minutes or until slightly thickened. Beat until frothy; fold in tuna (flaked). Chill in 4 oiled individual molds to firmness. Serve with salad greens. (Serves 4)

IN ADVANCE: Make your mousse and cookies the day before. You could make the biscuits the day before too, if you expect to be pressed for time, but they will be better fresh baked. The dessert can be made several hours ahead of time.

THE OTHER RECIPES: Tahitian onion soup (page 83); cheese biscuits (page 88); tipsy pears and raspberries (page 131); chocolate nut bars (page 138).

SUBSTITUTIONS: Mushroom spinach soup or Creole soup for the Tahitian onion soup; any other fruit dessert and any cookies of your choice.

MENU

Tomato Cranberry Soup
CHICKEN VEGETABLE SALAD
Toasted Mushroom Sandwiches
Ginger Fruit Cup
Oatmeal Cookies

* * *

COMMENTS: You will get compliments from the unusual soup (my invention), the delicious mushroom sandwiches, and the intriguing ginger-flavored fruit. Many people have never heard of ginger brandy.

CHICKEN VEGETABLE SALAD

2 cups diced cooked chicken   ½ cup diced celery
2 tablespoons lemon juice   ¼ cup chopped green pepper
2 tablespoons corn oil   ½ cup grated raw zucchini
¼ cup dairy sour cream   Lettuce
1 teaspoon onion salt   8 cherry tomatoes, halved
1 teaspoon paprika

Mix chicken with lemon juice, oil, sour cream, and seasonings; chill in covered container. Just before serving, mix in celery, green pepper, and zucchini. Serve on lettuce and garnish with halved cherry tomatoes. Pass EIDERDOWN DRESSING. (Serves 4)

IN ADVANCE: Cook chicken the day before if you have none on hand to dice. Prepare the fruit cup, since the ginger brandy will preserve the freshness of the fruit. Make cookies, if not already made. On the morning of the party make salad dressing. Fix mushroom sandwiches and refrigerate in covered container. Start baking them a few minutes before your serving time.

THE OTHER RECIPES: Tomato cranberry soup (page 78); toasted mushroom sandwiches (page 92); ginger fruit cup (page 132); oatmeal cookies (page 137).

SUBSTITUTIONS: Mushroom mini buns (page 93); any other fruit dessert.

MENU

Spinach Soup Tamaaraa
Sesame Crackers
CURRIED CHICKEN SALAD
Strawberry Banana Nut Bread
Celestial Sherry Cream

* * *

COMMENTS: An especially delicious lunch, starting with that unusual soup, reminiscent of Tahiti. The salad is pretty, with its yellow dressing, green grapes surrounding each portion like a necklace, and the egg white topping. It's tasty and crunchy, too. The strawberry banana bread is out of this world, and you'll end up on cloud nine with the soft luscious sherry dessert.

CURRIED CHICKEN SALAD

1½ cup diced cooked chicken
3 tablespoons lemon juice
½ teaspoon onion salt
½ teaspoon garlic salt
2 hard-cooked egg yolks
¼ cup dairy sour cream
¼ cup yogurt
1 teaspoon curry powder (or more)

¼ teaspoon turmeric
2 tablespoons corn oil
½ cup finely diced celery
¼ cup toasted sliced almonds
1 hard-cooked egg white, chopped very fine
Seedless green grapes *

* *If grapes are canned, use 20 (5 for each serving). If fresh, cut each in half and use 12 (6 halves for each serving).*

Soak chicken in lemon juice with onion and garlic salt at least 1 hour. Mash hard-cooked egg yolks with a fork and mix in sour cream until smooth. Mix in yogurt, curry powder, turmeric, and oil. Add to chicken with celery and almonds. Serve on shredded lettuce and surround with grapes. Put a dab of the chopped egg white on top of each serving. (Serves 4)

IN ADVANCE: Bake your bread the day before and make your dessert. (Both will then have time to ripen their flavors.) Cook a chicken and dice it for your salad, unless you already have some prepared. Morning of the party—hard-cook your eggs; dice celery; toast almonds; fix chicken to soak; thaw spinach. The rest is quick and easy.

THE OTHER RECIPES: Spinach soup Tamaaraa (page 85); strawberry banana nut bread (page 87); celestial sherry cream (page 134).

SUBSTITUTIONS: Mushroom spinach soup; banana bread; pear Bavarian.

MENU

Salmon Soup
MOLDED CHICKEN PINEAPPLE SALAD
Coconut Muffins
Strawberry Sherbet
Almond Cookies

*   *   *

COMMENTS: This is a satisfying menu, but not too rich for weight watchers—unless they eat a lot of those delicious coconut muffins!

MOLDED CHICKEN PINEAPPLE SALAD

1 envelope gelatin
1¾ cups chicken stock,
   divided
½ teaspoon onion salt
2 tablespoons lemon juice
EIDERDOWN PINEAPPLE
   DRESSING

1½ cups diced cooked
   chicken
½ cup drained canned
   crushed pineapple
½ cup diced celery
Salad greens
Seedless green grapes

Sprinkle gelatin on ¾ cup chicken stock; stir over low heat until dissolved. Remove from heat and stir in 1 cup chicken stock and remaining ingredients. Chill in 4 oiled individual molds until firm. Unmold on greens and garnish with grapes. Pass EIDERDOWN PINEAPPLE DRESSING. (Serves 4)

IN ADVANCE: You can make everything but the soup the day before—cheers! All you have to do the morning of your luncheon is fix salad greens and dressing (but you can even do that the day before).

THE OTHER RECIPES: Salmon soup (page 85); coconut muffins (page 90); strawberry sherbet (page 119); almond cookies (page 138).

SUBSTITUTIONS: Mushroom spinach soup or mushroom broth for the salmon soup; royal purple ice cream or raspberry sherry bisque for the strawberry sherbet.

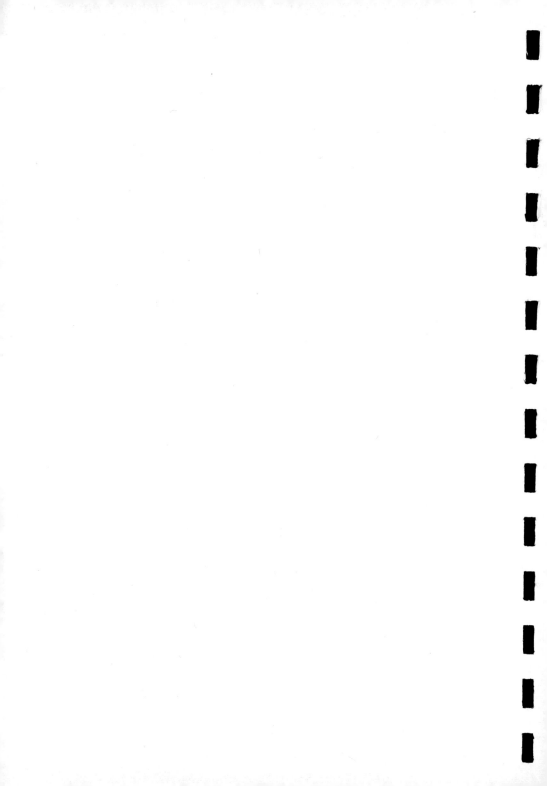

part II

dinners for eight

**meat dinners
chicken dinners
seafood dinners**

MENU

Tomato Cranberry Broth
BEEF STROGANOFF
Green Noodles (or rice)
Artichoke Celery Salad
Grape Pear Sherbet
Chocolate Nut Bars

* * *

COMMENTS: Beef stroganoff is always popular. What makes my version extra delicious is the magic ingredient—mustard—which enhances the flavor. This is a good entree to serve and keep warm in a chafing dish at a buffet dinner.

BEEF STROGANOFF

½ cup margarine	Dash of ground pepper
½ cup minced onion	¼ teaspoon garlic powder
1 pound sliced mushrooms	1 teaspoon dry mustard
2 pounds round steak, cut in ½-inch strips	2 tablespoons tomato paste
¼ cup flour	1 cup beef consommé
1 teaspoon salt	⅔ cup cream sherry
	1 cup dairy sour cream

Melt margarine and sauté onion about 10 minutes over low heat; add mushrooms. Cover and continue cooking 5 minutes. Remove onion and mushrooms to a bowl. Brown meat in same skillet over low heat, then blend in flour and seasonings. Add mushrooms, onion, tomato paste, consommé, and half of the sherry. Simmer gently about 1 hour. Just before serving stir in sour cream and remaining sherry. (Serves 8).

THE OTHER RECIPES: Tomato cranberry broth (page 78); artichoke celery salad (page 102); grape pear sherbet (page 132); chocolate nut bars (page 138).

SUBSTITUTIONS: Any other clear soup; any other vegetable salad; any other fruit or non-creamy dessert; any other cookie recipe.

MENU

SUKIYAKI
Rice
Pea Pods
Grapefruit Avocado Salad
Raspberry Sherry Mousse

* * *

COMMENTS: Another perfect entree to serve in a chafing dish or electric skillet. To carry out the oriental theme we add peapods, which can be bought packaged frozen and quickly cooked. That mousse is heavenly, yet so simple to make.

SUKIYAKI

3 tablespoons safflower oil	1 tablespoon maple syrup
2 lbs. sirloin steak, 1 inch thick	1 teaspoon ginger
¼ cup thin-sliced celery	1 can (6 oz.) water chestnuts, sliced
1 tablespoon cornstarch	1 can (4 oz.) sliced mushrooms
⅓ cup bouillon	
¼ cup soy sauce	8 green onions with 1 inch of stems, sliced
½ cup sherry	

Freeze steak 1 hour, then slice in ⅛-inch slices. In hot skillet sauté meat and celery in the oil until meat is browned. In small bowl stir cornstarch into bouillon; add to beef mixture. Cook, stirring, until thick and clear. Add remaining ingredients and simmer until well heated. Diced cooked pork or chicken can be substituted for part of the beef. (Serves 8)

IN ADVANCE: The dessert can be made a day or more before your party and frozen. About 1½ hours before dinner time freeze the steak (see recipe instructions). The salad can be prepared about an hour in advance, if you dip the avocado slices in lemon juice to prevent discoloring.

THE OTHER RECIPES: Grapefruit avocado salad (page 100); raspberry sherry mousse (page 121).

SUBSTITUTIONS: Any other salad; any other dessert.

MENU

MARINATED FLANK STEAK
Savory Baked Potatoes
Green Beans and Almonds
Caesar Salad
Caramel Cacao Frozen Pears
Pecan Pie Cookies

* * *

COMMENTS: Many people like flank steak as well as sirloin, and it is a lot cheaper. This sweet-sour version is delicious. And that dessert is yummy! You'll wonder why you never had it before.

MARINATED FLANK STEAK

⅓ cup soy sauce
3 tablespoons vinegar
3 tablespoons maple syrup
⅓ cup safflower oil

2 teaspoons onion powder
1 flank steak (about 2
   pounds), scored

Combine first 5 ingredients in flat Tupperware container. Marinate the flank steak in this marinade several hours or overnight, turning over several times. Broil about 4 minutes on each side. Slice diagonally. (Serves 8)

IN ADVANCE: Marinate the flank steak overnight, if possible. Dice your canned pears for the dessert and freeze them at least several hours before dinner time. The potatoes can be fixed in advance and warmed up during the last few minutes.

THE OTHER RECIPES: Savory baked potatoes (page 96); caramel cacao frozen pears (page 117); pecan pie cookies (page 141).

SUBSTITUTIONS: Any other green vegetable; any other simple salad; any other fruity dessert; any other cookies.

MENU

Spinach Broth
BAKED HAM
Guava Sweet Potatoes
Tomato Artichoke Salad
Aqua Fruit Cup
Chocolate Coconut Cookies

* * *

COMMENTS: Baked ham may be very ordinary, but the exotic sweet potatoes certainly are not. I usually cook bananas in them, but this is more of a surprise—and heavenly. The fruit cup is a surprise too. It's likely that none of your friends has ever seen a dessert this color before. Definitely gourmet.

BAKED HAM

1 can (3 pounds) cooked ham

Remove ham from can. Heat in a 300° oven about 30 minutes. Serve sliced. (Serves 8 or more)

IN ADVANCE: Salad dressing must be made the day before, and the cookies may be. You can cook your sweet potatoes ahead of time and have them ready, either for the casserole or to heat with the jelly almost at the last minute. Cut up the fruit for your dessert and chill in covered container at least 2 hours before serving.

THE OTHER RECIPES:
Spinach broth (page 81);
guava sweet potatoes (page
98); tomato artichoke salad
(page 102); aqua fruit cup
(page 130); chocolate coconut
cookies (page 137).

SUBSTITUTIONS: Any other
vegetable salad; any other
fruit dessert; any other
cookies.

MENU

LAMB CURRY
Rice
Banana Peas
Eggplant Casserole
Grapefruit Cherry Fruit Cup
Best Ever Lemon Cookies

* * *

COMMENTS: Curried dishes are definitely company fare. Peas seem to be the traditional vegetable to go with lamb, but I give them a new twist—just for fun. Since peas are quite sweet, why not add a bit more sweetness to them? Especially since something sweet is always served with curry. Cooked bananas make them almost exotic. Eggplant teams with lamb in the Near East, so we are also adding that to this menu.

LAMB CURRY

2 tablespoons margarine
2 large onions, chopped
2 tablespoons flour
¾ teaspoon garlic salt
2 teaspoons curry powder
2 teaspoons turmeric

½ teaspoon ground ginger
2 cups consommé
4 cups cooked cubed lamb
   (about 2 pounds)
½ cup yogurt

Melt margarine in skillet; sauté onion till golden. Stir in next 5 ingredients; heat briefly. Add consommé gradually, cooking and stirring until thick. Add lamb, and simmer till well heated. Just before serving stir in yogurt. (Serves 8)

IN ADVANCE: You can cook your lamb ahead of time, cut it in cubes, and refrigerate it until ready to start the recipe. The cookies can be made the day before.

THE OTHER RECIPES: Banana peas (page 98); eggplant casserole (page 97); grapefruit cherry fruit cup (page 135); best ever lemon cookies (page 141).

SUBSTITUTIONS: Any other fruit dessert; any other cookies.

MENU

Vichyssoise Verte
VEAL VOLGA
Mashed Potatoes
Mushroom Spinach Bake
Tossed Salad
June Fruit Sherbet
Almond Crumb Cookies

*   *   *

COMMENTS: The soup isn't really necessary on this balanced menu, but if you're feeling ambitious you might like to include it. This veal inspiration is extra special! Some Palm Beach friends of ours serve it at every dinner party. So if you want to impress someone, this is your dish. By way of contrast, the vegetables and salad are simple and not sweet.

VEAL VOLGA

½ cup minced onion
½ cup margarine
2 pounds thin veal steak,
  cut in 1-inch strips
4 tablespoons flour
1 teaspoon salt
Dash ground pepper
1 teaspoon dry mustard

¼ cup soy sauce
¼ cup ginger brandy
1 cup bouillon or consommé
1 cup orange wine
¼ cup orange marmalade
¼ cup orange liqueur
  (Cointreau, curaçao, etc.)
1 cup dairy sour cream

In a Dutch oven or large covered skillet sauté onion in margarine until golden, then push aside and add veal. Brown well on both sides; add flour, seasonings, soy sauce, ginger brandy, half of the bouillon (or consommé), and part of the orange wine. Simmer, covered, for 1 hour, adding more wine and bouillon when it gets dry. Lastly, mix in the marmalade, orange liqueur, and sour cream. Heat to boiling, but do not allow to boil. (Serves 8)

IN ADVANCE: Make the sherbet and cookies the day before, if possible.

THE OTHER RECIPES: Vichyssoise verte (page 80); mushroom spinach bake (page 97); June fruit sherbet (page 121); almond crumb cookies (page 142).

SUBSTITUTIONS: Any other green vegetable; any other fruit dessert; any other cookies.

MENU

CURRIED PINEAPPLE CHICKEN
Rice
Tipsy Banana Carrots
Tahitian Spinach
Guava Grapefruit Coupe
Oatmeal Cookies

* * *

COMMENTS: A perfect menu for a Hawaiian party—with Polynesian fruits and coconut added, even to the vegetables. Your guests will rave about that unusual spinach!

CURRIED PINEAPPLE CHICKEN

1 cup chopped onion
2 tablespoons margarine
2 teaspoons curry powder
1 cup crushed pineapple
¼ cup frozen pineapple
    juice concentrate

3½ cups cooked diced chicken
1 can condensed cream of
    chicken soup
½ cup unsweetened coconut
    meal*
½ cup dairy sour cream

*available in health food stores

Sauté onion in the margarine until soft; stir in curry powder and cook for half a minute. Add remaining ingredients, except sour cream. Simmer until ready to serve (or heat in casserole in oven), then stir in sour cream. (Serves 8)

IN ADVANCE: Cook your chicken the day before, and remove meat from bones while still warm. Refrigerate in covered container. Bake cookies the day before or morning of party. Chill the fruit cup at least 2 hours before dinner time.

THE OTHER RECIPES: Tipsy banana carrots (page 95); Tahitian spinach (page 95); guava grapefruit coupe (page 131); oatmeal cookies (page 137).

SUBSTITUTIONS: Any other fruit dessert; any other cookie recipe.

MENU

BANANA BRANDY CHICKEN
Rice
Italian Green Beans and Mushrooms
Grapefruit Zucchini Salad
Danish Pear Mold
Coffee Cookies

*   *   *

COMMENTS: All that booze gives this dish great zest and extra deliciousness. It may sound wild, but watch your guests go for second helpings!

BANANA BRANDY CHICKEN

⅓ cup banana liqueur *
3 tablespoons brandy
3 tablespoons vodka
½ cup dairy sour cream
⅓ cup chopped onion
1 tablespoon margarine
1½ cups mashed ripe
   banana

2 tablespoons lemon juice
¾ cup condensed cream of
   chicken soup
2 teaspoons chicken bouillon
   granules (optional)
½ teaspoon salt
3½ cups diced cooked chicken

*Leroux brand recommended

With a wire whisk, combine the first 4 ingredients, and refrigerate for several hours or overnight. About ½ hour before serving time, sauté onion in the margarine, add mashed banana, and cook 5 minutes. Add lemon juice, soup, bouillon granules, and salt; cook a few minutes. Add chicken and heat gently until serving time. When taken from heat, stir in reserved brandy mixture. (Do not cook again!) This could be heated in a casserole in the oven if you wish to serve it in a casserole. (Serves 8)

IN ADVANCE: Cook chicken the day before. The dessert and cookies can be made the day before or morning of the party. Chill salad ingredients at least 2 hours before dinner time.

THE OTHER RECIPES: Grapefruit zucchini salad (page 100); Danish pear mold (page 126); coffee cookies (page 140).

SUBSTITUTIONS: Any other green vegetable; any other salad; any other molded fruit dessert; any other cookie recipe.

MENU

PINEAPPLE WINE CHICKEN
Rice
Peas and Water Chestnuts
Mushroom Spinach Bake
Purple Parfait
Chewy Cinnamon Cookies

* * *

COMMENTS: A delicious and unusual chicken dish—quite tantalizing. Fine for people who can't eat onion (no onion in the entire menu). Watch them go for that tasty spinach! You won't have many cookies left, either—these are the nonstop variety.

PINEAPPLE WINE CHICKEN

1 cup pineapple wine *
⅔ cup dairy sour cream
1 can condensed cream of
   chicken soup

⅔ cup frozen pineapple
   juice concentrate
3½ cups diced cooked
   chicken

*Mardi Gras brand recommended

Several hours or the day before serving, beat wine and sour cream together with a wire whisk; refrigerate in tightly covered container.

Combine soup, pineapple juice, and diced chicken in large casserole; heat in oven about 25 minutes at 350°. Just before serving, stir in reserved wine mixture. (Serves 8)

IN ADVANCE: Cook chicken the day before or morning of party and refrigerate the diced meat. Also bake cookies ahead of time. Refrigerate the combined wine and sour cream. The jellied dessert must have ample time to jell and chill.

THE OTHER RECIPES: Mushroom spinach bake (page 97); purple parfait (page 129); chewy cinnamon cookies (page 139).

SUBSTITUTIONS: Any other vegetables; any other fruit dessert; any other cookie recipe.

MENU

BANANA GRAND MARNIER CHICKEN
Rice
Pineapple Carrots
Artichoke Celery Salad
Lemon Pudding
Chewy Bread-Crumb Macaroons

* * *

COMMENTS: A very elegant chicken recipe—bananas and orange are a delicious duo. Even carrot-haters will love those carrots, and everybody likes lemon desserts.

BANANA GRAND MARNIER CHICKEN

½ cup Grand Marnier
  liqueur
½ cup dairy sour cream
2 tablespoons margarine
½ cup chopped onion
1 can condensed cream of
  chicken soup

2 cups mashed ripe bananas
½ cup frozen orange juice
  concentrate
¼ cup lemon juice
3½ cups diced cooked
  chicken

Several hours in advance, or the night before, beat together Grand Marnier and sour cream with wire whisk; refrigerate in covered container until serving time.

Melt margarine in large skillet; sauté onion until limp. Stir in soup, mashed banana, orange and lemon juices. Transfer to large casserole and bake at 350° for at least half an hour. Add chicken, and bake 20-30 minutes longer. Just before serving, stir in reserved sour cream mixture. (Serves 8)

IN ADVANCE: Cook chicken the day before or morning of party, likewise the cookies. Lemon pudding needs chilling, so it can be made early in the day.

THE OTHER RECIPES: Pineapple carrots (page 94); artichoke celery salad (page 102); lemon pudding (page 136); chewy bread-crumb macaroons (page 142).

SUBSTITUTIONS: Any other vegetable salad; any other dessert or cookies.

MENU

GINGER PINEAPPLE CHICKEN
Rice
Zucchini Majorca
Curried Avocado Mold
Peach Almond Dream
Almond Cookies

* * *

COMMENTS: Ginger makes this entree interesting and unusual. The comment on my recipe card says, "Divine!" That dessert is celestial, too, if you like almond flavor—and most people do. Almond cookies team up well with it.

GINGER PINEAPPLE CHICKEN

¼ cup brandy
½ cup vodka
½ cup dairy sour cream
½ cup chopped onion
2 tablespoons margarine
2 tablespoons flour
½ cup milk
¼ cup juice drained from
  can of pineapple
4 teaspoons soy sauce

¾ teaspoon salt
1 can condensed cream of
  chicken soup
3½ cups diced cooked chicken
⅓ cup ginger marmalade
2 cans (8 oz. each) pine-
  apple chunks in
  unsweetened juice, cut up
¼ cup toasted sliced almonds

Combine brandy, vodka, and sour cream; refrigerate in covered container several hours. Sauté onion in the margarine until soft; stir in flour, then add milk and pineapple juice gradually. Cook until thick. Add soy sauce, salt, and soup; cook for a few minutes. Stir in chicken, ginger marmalade, and diced pineapple; heat well. Just before serving, stir in reserved brandy mixture and remove from heat immediately. Serve sprinkled with sliced almonds. (Serves 8).

IN ADVANCE: Cook chickens the day before or morning of party; also the cookies. The salad and dessert can be chilled way in advance. Such an easy dessert! The liqueur keeps the peaches from discoloring.

THE OTHER RECIPES: Zucchini Majorca (page 98); curried avocado mold (page 104); peach almond dream (page 133); almond cookies (page 138).

SUBSTITUTIONS: Any other vegetable and salad; any other fruit dessert; any other cookies.

MENU

Quick Mushroom Broth
PINEAPPLE BANANA CHICKEN
Rice
Vegetable Medley
Tropical Rum Fruit Cup
Anise Cookies

* * *

COMMENTS: Another of my "tipsy" recipes. Liqueurs, or any kind of alcoholic beverage, add great zest to food, especially when accompanied by fruit. With this vegetable medley, there is no need for salad in addition. You don't often see (or think of) anise cookies. Delicious!

PINEAPPLE BANANA CHICKEN

½ cup pineapple wine*
⅓ cup banana liqueur **
⅔ cup dairy sour cream
2 tablespoons frozen pineapple juice concentrate
2 cups mashed ripe bananas

2 tablespoons lemon juice
1 can condensed cream of
chicken soup
3½ cups diced cooked
chicken
½ teaspoon salt

*Mardi Gras brand recommended
**Leroux brand recommended

In advance: combine wine, liqueur, and sour cream with wire whisk; refrigerate in covered container several hours or overnight. About 45 minutes before serving, combine pineapple juice, mashed banana, lemon juice, soup, chicken, and salt. Bake in greased casserole, covered, at 350° for about 30 minutes. After removing from oven, stir in reserved sour cream mixture. (Serves 8)

IN ADVANCE: Cook chickens and remove from bones the day before, or morning of party, and refrigerate. Bake cookies in advance, too. As instructed in recipe, mix wine, liqueur, and sour cream, and refrigerate several hours or overnight.

THE OTHER RECIPES: Quick mushroom broth (page 79); vegetable medley (page 94); tropical rum fruit cup (page 132); anise cookies (page 143).

SUBSTITUTIONS: Any other two vegetables, or one vegetable and a salad instead of vegetable medley; any other fruit dessert; any other cookies.

MENU

Carrot Banana Soup
CURRIED SHRIMP
Rice
Green Ball Salad
Pecan Crunch Ice Cream

*   *   *

COMMENTS: Who ever heard of such a crazy soup? But bananas go well with curry, so it isn't so absurd after all. There's more fruit in the salad—all to the good. Pretty, too, with that fluffy green dressing. You won't need cookies: that nutty ice cream has them in it.

CURRIED SHRIMP

1 cup chopped onion	3½ cups cooked shrimp
2 teaspoons margarine	(cut up, if large)
1 teaspoon curry powder	1 cup dairy sour cream
1 can condensed cream of	Paprika
shrimp soup	

Sauté onion in the margarine until tender, but not brown; stir in curry powder and cook about ½ minute. Add soup and shrimp; cook about 1 minute (if shrimp is frozen, cook a little longer). Stir in sour cream and paprika. Heat, but do not boil. (Serves 8)

IN ADVANCE: The ice cream should be made the day before. You can fix your salad (scoop out the balls) several hours in advance and chill.

THE OTHER RECIPES: Carrot banana soup (page 84); green ball salad (page 101); pecan crunch ice cream (page 116).

SUBSTITUTIONS: Any other fruit and vegetable salad; any other dessert.

MENU

Spicy Tomato Rhubarb Soup
SHRIMP CELERY CASSEROLE
Rice
Curaçao Carrots
Purple Pineapple Mold

* * *

COMMENTS: This casserole dish is crunchy, flavorful, but not rich or creamy. Because it is not baked too long, the celery and green pepper retain their flavor and crispness. Everyone will want the recipe for those carrots! Delightful! You don't need another vegetable or salad because there are two vegetables in the casserole. The dessert is refreshing and not too sweet.

SHRIMP CELERY CASSEROLE

4 teaspoons margarine
1 cup chopped onion
1 garlic clove, minced
1 cup condensed celery soup
½ cup dairy sour cream
½ cup chopped celery
⅔ cup chopped green pepper
4 cups frozen cooked shrimp

½ teaspoon garlic salt
Dash ground pepper
¼ teaspoon bouquet garni
   (or thyme)
¼ cup toasted sliced
   almonds
1 cup buttered cracker
   crumbs

Sauté onion and garlic in the margarine, separated, in skillet. Remove garlic when it starts to turn golden. Stir in remaining ingredients, except nuts and crumbs. Put in greased casserole and sprinkle with nuts and crumbs. Bake at 350° about 25-30 minutes (no longer). (Serves 8)

IN ADVANCE: The dessert should be made several hours in advance to jell and chill.

THE OTHER RECIPES: Spicy tomato rhubarb soup (page 78); curaçao (page 95); purple pineapple mold (page 127).

SUBSTITUTIONS: Any other thin soup; any other fruity dessert.

MENU

CURRIED SEAFOOD CASSEROLE
Rice
Sherry Baked Onions
Fruit and Vegetable Salad
Coffee Dream Cream
Lace Cookies

*   *   *

COMMENTS: Everyone will consider this menu a great treat, with 4 varieties of seafood in the creamy curried casserole. Wait till they taste those sherried onions! Wow! The coffee dessert is a smooth and proper finale, accompanied by fragile cookies.

CURRIED SEAFOOD CASSEROLE

½ cup chopped onion	½ cup diced lobster
1 tablespoon margarine	1 cup crabmeat
1 tablespoon curry powder	1 can cream of shrimp soup
1 cup cut-up scallops	1 cup dairy sour cream
1 cup large shrimp	½ teaspoon salt

Sauté onion in the margarine until limp; add curry, cook about 2 minutes, and set it aside. Drop scallops into boiling water and boil 3 minutes. Drain and add shrimp, lobster, crabmeat, soup, sour cream, and salt. Bake in a greased casserole at 350° about 30 minutes. (Serves 8)

IN ADVANCE: The cookies can be made a day ahead. The dessert can be chilled several hours before dinner.

SUBSTITUTIONS: Any other vegetable; any other fruit and vegetable salad; any other dessert; any other cookies.

THE OTHER RECIPES: Sherry baked onions (page 96); fruit and vegetable salad (page 101); coffee dream cream (page 134); lace cookies (page 140).

MENU

Quick Mushroom Broth
OYSTERS AND CRAB AU GRATIN
Green Noodles
Raw Vegetable Salad
Rum Fruit Compote
Coffee Macaroons

* * *

COMMENTS: The soup isn't really necessary—but nice. Seafood lovers will dote on this elegant casserole; it's expensive, but worth it. We end with a sophisticated fruit dessert and unusual cookies.

OYSTERS AND CRAB AU GRATIN

2 cans (7 oz. each) or
24 fresh oysters
⅓ cup margarine
4 teaspoons minced onion
¼ cup flour
1½ cups milk

1 cup grated cheese
2 cups crabmeat, defrosted
1 egg yolk
¼ tablespoon dairy sour
cream
¾ cup dry bread crumbs
1½ tablespoons soft butter

Cook oysters in their liquid until edges curl. Melt margarine and sauté onion about 3 minutes. Stir in flour, then milk gradually; cook until thick. Add cheese, and stir until melted. Mix in cooked oysters and the crabmeat, then egg yolk and sour cream. Spoon into a greased casserole. Mix crumbs with the soft butter; sprinkle on top. Bake in hot oven just until well heated. (Serves 8)

IN ADVANCE: Cookies can be made a day ahead. Freeze fruits for your dessert either the day before or morning of your party. The salad dressing and some of the vegetables can be prepared ahead of time.

THE OTHER RECIPES: Quick mushroom broth (page 79); raw vegetable salad (page 103); rum fruit compote (page 117); coffee macaroons (page 140).

SUBSTITUTIONS: Any other thin broth; rice for the green noodles; any other vegetable salad; any other fruit dessert; any other cookies.

MENU

SCALLOPED SALMON
Mashed Potatoes
Grapefruit Vegetable Salad
Apricot Sherbet
Candy Cookie Bars

* * *

COMMENTS: Since peas go so well with salmon, I am including them in the salad—raw, but delicious. It's time you got acquainted with them that way!

SCALLOPED SALMON

¼ cup margarine
6 tablespoons minced onion
¼ cup flour
Dash garlic salt
2 cups milk

2 cans (7 ¾ oz. each) red salmon
1 egg, beaten
⅔ cup cracker crumbs
4 teaspoons butter

Melt margarine and sauté onion until tender; stir in flour and garlic salt, then add milk slowly while stirring. Bring to boil and cook 3 minutes while stirring. Remove skin from salmon; add salmon (flaked with a fork) to cream sauce along with its bones and liquid. Fold in beaten egg. Bake in greased casserole covered with buttered crumbs about 35 minutes at 350°. (Serves 8)

THE OTHER RECIPES: Grapefruit vegetable salad (page 103); apricot sherbet (page 125); candy cookie bars (page 143).

SUBSTITUTIONS: Raw vegetable salad or green ball salad for the grapefruit vegetable salad; any other fruit dessert; any other cookies.

MENU

TUNA OLIVE CASSEROLE
Savory Baked Potatoes
Peas
Caesar Salad
June Fruit Sherbet
Pecan Crisp Cookies

* * *

COMMENTS: With meat and most seafood prices soaring, people are now hoping for ways to make tuna interesting company fare. I think you'll agree that this is a good example. The whole menu is very simple and plebeian, but men especially will like it. These cookies are extra-special delights (my husband's favorites), so your meal will end up with happy faces and pleasant memories.

TUNA OLIVE CASSEROLE

1 cup chopped onion	¾ teaspoon garlic salt
2 tablespoons margarine	Dash ground pepper
2 cups chopped green pepper	2 cans (7 oz. each) tuna,
2 tablespoons flour	drained, if packed in oil
1 cup milk (or more)	24 pimiento-stuffed olives

Melt margarine, and sauté onion and green pepper until tender. Mix in flour, then milk gradually. Cook over low heat about 5 minutes; add garlic salt, pepper, tuna, and chopped olives. Heat in casserole about 25 minutes at 350°, or simmer in saucepan over low heat about 10 minutes, adding more milk if it gets too dry. (Serves 8)

IN ADVANCE: The sherbet and cookies can be made a day ahead.

THE OTHER RECIPES: Savory baked potatoes (page 96); June fruit sherbet (page 121); pecan crisp cookies (page 139).

SUBSTITUTIONS: Any other green vegetable; any other salad; any other fruit dessert; any other cookies.

part III

other recipes and substitutions

soups
breads
vegetables
vegetable salad
fruit salads
salad dressings
desserts
cookies

index

SPICY TOMATO RHUBARB BROTH

Another interesting vegetable broth to offset your creamy salad.

½ cup diced fresh rhubarb
2 cups tomato juice

¼ teaspoon powdered cloves

Cook the diced rhubarb in the tomato juice with powdered cloves until soft. Run in blender until smooth. Serve hot. (Serves 4)

TOMATO CRANBERRY BROTH

Cranberries add the tartness of lemon juice—not sour, just zesty.

2 cups tomato juice

⅓ cup raw cranberries

Run about half of the tomato juice in blender with cranberries until liquified. Pour into saucepan, add remaining juice, and heat to boiling. Serve with a dollop of yogurt in each bowl, floating on top of soup, if desired. (Serves 4)

CREOLE SOUP

1 tablespoon margarine
¼ cup chopped onion
¼ cup chopped green
  pepper
1¼ cups tomato juice

⅛ teaspoon oregano
½ teaspoon garlic salt
¼ cup (or more) chicken
  stock
8 pimiento-stuffed olives,
  cut up

Sauté onion and green pepper in the margarine 5 minutes; add tomato juice, oregano, and garlic salt; simmer 15 minutes. Run in blender until smooth. Pour into pint measuring pitcher; add chicken stock to measure 1 pint. Return to saucepan and heat briefly; stir in chopped olives. (Serves 4)

CLEAR GREEK LEMON SOUP

1 can chicken broth
¼ cup lemon juice

½ cup water
2 eggs, well beaten

Heat broth and water to boiling; add lemon juice. Remove from heat and gradually add to beaten eggs. Pour into saucepan and heat, stirring until it starts to get thick. Do not boil! (Serves 4)

QUICK MUSHROOM BROTH

¼ cup beef flavor mushroom
  soup mix
2½ cups water

½ teaspoon onion (or
  garlic) salt

Bring ingredients to a boil, then lower heat and simmer 3 minutes. (Serves 4)

VICHYSSOISE VERTE

¾ cup condensed cream
  of potato soup
½ cup raw peas
¼ cup yogurt

2 tablespoons dairy sour
  cream
1 cup milk
1 tablespoon frozen
  chopped chives

Boil soup and peas together 3 minutes; cool. Dump into blender with remaining ingredients; run until smooth. Serve well chilled. (Serves 4)

STRAWBERRY BORSCH

½ cup finely diced cooked
  beets (fresh or canned)
6 tablespoons beet juice
½ cup water
½ cup chopped strawberries
2 tablespoons finely minced radishes

½ teaspoon salt
¼ cup strawberry wine
½ cup yogurt (or dairy
  sour cream)

Run first 6 ingredients in blender until smooth. Transfer to saucepan and cook 3 minutes. Remove from heat and add wine. Blend in yogurt (or sour cream) with wire whisk. Pour into pint measuring pitcher and add water to measure 2 cups. Serve well chilled. (Serves 4)

MUSHROOM SPINACH SOUP

¼ package frozen chopped spinach,   2 cups water
   thawed, but not drained
2½ tablespoons beef flavor mushroom soup mix

Simmer about 3 minutes, then run in blender until smooth. (Serves 4)

SPINACH BROTH

½ package frozen chopped   1 can consommé
   spinach   2 tablespoons lemon juice

Thoroughly thaw spinach; do not drain. Put in blender with part of the consommé; run until smooth. Pour into saucepan, add remaining consommé and lemon juice, heat just to boiling point. (Serves 4).

CURAÇAO BEET SOUP

1½ cups diced canned beets   2 tablespoons dairy sour
   and juice   cream
3 tablespoons frozen orange   ¼ teaspoon salt
   juice concentrate   ¼ teaspoon dry mustard
¼ cup yogurt   3 tablespoons curaçao

Put beets and juice with remaining ingredients, except curaçao, in blender; run until smooth. Transfer to saucepan; heat, but do not let boil. When ready to serve, stir in curaçao. Serve hot. (Serves 4)

BANANA PEA SOUP

½ cup cooked peas
½ cup cooking water from peas
¼ cup mashed ripe banana

1½ cups milk
½ teaspoon salt
1 tablespoon butter

Run peas and their cooking water with mashed banana in blender until smooth. Transfer to a saucepan and cook 3 minutes. Add milk and salt; heat to boiling, then stir in butter. (Serves 4)

MUSHROOM BROTH

⅓ cup chopped onion
2 tablespoons butter
   (clarified)
1¼ cups chopped fresh mushrooms

1¾ cups water
½ teaspoon seasoned salt
Dash pepper

Sauté onion in the clarified butter until limp; push aside (or remove), and sauté mushrooms until browned. Add part of the water, salt, and pepper; boil 5 minutes, then run in blender with remaining water. Pour into saucepan and heat to boiling just before serving. (Serves 4)

AVOCADO BANANA SOUP

⅓ cup frozen peas   ½ teaspoon salt
⅓ cup mashed ripe banana   ¼ cup dairy sour cream
1 cup mashed avocado   ⅓ cup coconut meal*
1 tablespoon lemon juice   Water to make 2 cups

* unsweetened—available at health food stores

Cook peas in small amount of water until tender; add mashed banana and cook 2 minutes. Dump in blender; add remaining ingredients; run until smooth. Pour into a quart measuring pitcher; add enough water to make 2 cups. Transfer to same saucepan; heat, but do not let boil. Serve hot or cold. (Serve with tiny fish crackers in miniature lotus bowls.) (Serves 4)

TAHITIAN ONION SOUP

4 medium-large onions   ¼ cup unsweetened
6 tablespoons mashed   coconut meal *
   ripe banana   ½ teaspoon hickory-
¼ cup dairy sour cream   smoked salt
1½ cups milk

*is available at health food stores

Slice onions and cook until tender in small amount of water; drain. Add mashed banana, and cook 3 minutes. Run in blender with sour cream and milk until smooth. Return to saucepan, add coconut meal mixed with the smoked salt; heat, but do not allow to boil. (Serves 4)

CARROT BANANA SOUP

3 medium carrots, scraped
  and sliced
1½ cups water
2 tablespoons lemon juice
½ tablespoon frozen orange
  juice concentrate

⅔ cup mashed ripe banana
¼ teaspoon salt
2 teaspoons butter
3 tablespoons Cointreau

Cook carrots in the water until tender; drain cooking water into pint pitcher; add water to measure 1½ cups. Dump into blender with carrots, lemon juice, orange juice, and mashed banana; run until smooth. Pour into saucepan, add salt, and cook 2 minutes. Remove from heat and stir in butter and Cointreau. (Serves 4)

ORANGE WINE CARROT SOUP

3 medium carrots, scraped
  and sliced
¼ cup orange wine
2 tablespoons lemon juice
¼ teaspoon salt

½ tablespoon frozen orange
  juice concentrate
2 tablespoons Cointreau (or
  any orange liqueur)
1 tablespoon butter

Cook carrots in small amount of water until tender. Drain cooking water into a pint pitcher; add orange wine and enough water to measure 1½ cups liquid. Put carrots with part of the liquid in blender and run until smooth. Pour into saucepan, add lemon juice, salt, and orange juice; heat. Just before serving, add Cointreau and butter. Decorate with carrot curls, if desired. (Serves 4)

SALMON SOUP

1 tablespoon margarine	2 tablespoons tomato paste
¼ cup chopped onion	1 can (7¾ oz.) red
2 teaspoons flour	salmon
½ teaspoon Lawry's garlic salt	2 cups milk

Sauté onion in the margarine until limp; stir in flour and garlic salt, then some of the milk. Boil, stirring about 2 minutes; mix in tomato paste. Remove skin from salmon and flake with fork; add to onion mixture with remainder of milk. Dump into blender and run until smooth. Return to saucepan and cook about 2 minutes. (Serves 4)

SPINACH SOUP TAMAARAA

½ package frozen chopped spinach	¾ teaspoon hickory smoked salt
½ cup water	6 tablespoons unsweetened
Milk (about 1 cup)	coconut meal *
¼ cup dairy sour cream	
*available at health food stores	

Cook spinach briefly in the water. Dump into blender and run until smooth. Pour into a pint measuring pitcher and add enough milk to measure 2 cups. Pour into saucepan, beat in sour cream with wire whisk; stir in smoked salt and coconut meal. Heat just to boiling point. (Serves 4).

CONSOMMÉ SANGRIA

We enjoyed sangria in Spain, where it is almost the national drink. It is basically red wine and fruit juices—orange, lemon, lime, etc.—but every restaurant makes it differently, just as every family in India has its own curry recipe. You can find sangria in this country, even in supermarkets.

2 cups beef consommé
  (or broth)
4 teaspoons lemon juice

¼ cup sangria wine
Paper-thin celery slices

Heat broth and lemon juice to boiling. Just before serving stir in wine. Decorate with thin celery slices topped with a speck of parsley, if desired. (Serves 4)

AVOCADO GREEN SOUP

¾ cup mashed avocado
6 tablespoons chopped green
  pepper
1 sprig watercress
3 tablespoons lemon juice

½ cup yogurt
1¾ cups milk
¾ teaspoon garlic salt
2 tablespoons chopped
  chives

Run all ingredients in blender except chives, then stir in chives. Chill. (Serves 4)

STRAWBERRY BANANA NUT BREAD

Moist, red, and distractingly delicious.

2½ cups biscuit mix
1 package (3 oz.) strawberry
  gelatin
¼ cup sugar
1½ cups mashed ripe bananas
3 tablespoons lemon juice

1 egg, beaten
¾ cup cut-up fresh
  strawberries
¾ cup coarsely chopped,
  blanched almonds

Combine first 3 ingredients in large bowl. In another bowl mix remaining ingredients, then add to dry mixture. Beat until well mixed. Bake in greased loaf pan at 325° about 1 hour or until bread leaves sides of pan. Let cool in pan a few minutes before removing. (This is best when warm or toasted in the oven next day.)

BEST BANANA BREAD

½ cup margarine (1 stick)
½ cup brown sugar
½ cup granulated sugar
2 medium (or 1 extra
  large) eggs, beaten
2 tablespoons lemon juice

2 cups (5 or 6) mashed
  ripe bananas
2 cups flour
1 teaspoon soda
½ teaspoon salt

Cream margarine and sugars; add beaten eggs, lemon juice, and mashed banana. Combine flour, soda, and salt; beat into banana mixture. Bake in greased large loaf pan at 375° about 50-60 minutes until well browned.

ORANGE BREAD

This is delicious either hot or cold, and especially with honey.

2 tablespoons margarine
½ cup sugar
½ cup frozen orange juice
  concentrate
¼ cup hot water
Grated rind of 1 orange
1 tablespoon lemon juice

½ cup dairy sour cream
1 egg, beaten
2 cups flour
1½ teaspoons baking powder
½ teaspoon soda
¼ teaspoon salt

Cream together margarine and sugar. Mix frozen orange juice with hot water; add to creamed mixture. Add grated rind, lemon juice, and sour cream. Beat with wire whisk until smooth; fold in beaten egg. Combine dry ingredients; stir into orange mixture just until well combined. Bake in greased loaf pan at 350° about 50 minutes.

CHEESE BISCUITS

¾ cup all-purpose flour
1½ teaspoons baking powder
¼ teaspoon salt
½ teaspoon dry mustard

6 tablespoons grated sharp
  cheese
3 tablespoons margarine
6 tablespoons milk

Mix dry ingredients thoroughly; add grated cheese. Work in margarine with pastry blender. Quickly stir in milk with a fork to make a soft dough. With floured hands pat out dough on a floured board; roll or pat out to ¾" thickness. Cut with small biscuit cutter. Bake on ungreased cookie sheet at 450° about 10 minutes. (Makes 12 small biscuits)

PEANUT BACON BITS BISCUITS

¾ cup all-purpose flour   ¼ cup peanut butter
1½ teaspoons baking powder   ⅓ cup non-meat bacon
½ teaspoon onion salt   bits
¼ cup hard margarine   ⅓ cup milk

Proceed as for cheese biscuits, but add peanut butter to margarine, then bacon bits, and lastly milk.

SCALLION TOP BISCUITS

¾ cup flour   ¼ cup milk
1½ teaspoons baking powder   ⅓ cup minced green tops
½ teaspoon onion salt   of scallions
¼ cup hard margarine   2 teaspoons onion juice (or
                             finely grated onion)

Proceed as for cheese biscuits, adding scallion tops and onion juice (or grated onion) to dough.

WALNUT BISCUITS

¾ cup flour   ¼ cup hard margarine
1½ teaspoons baking powder   ¼ cup milk
½ teaspoon seasoned salt   ⅓ cup chopped walnuts

Proceed as for cheese biscuits, adding chopped walnuts to the dough.

BANANA BLUEBERRY MUFFINS

1⅓ cups biscuit mix
⅔ cup sugar
¼ teaspoon soda
1 egg
¾ cup blueberries

1 cup mashed ripe banana
1 tablespoon lemon juice
2 tablespoons margarine,
  melted

Heat oven to 375°. Mix dry ingredients in large bowl thoroughly; mix in remaining ingredients. Beat vigorously ½ minute. Fill greased muffin tins almost full. Bake at 375° for about 20 minutes, until very brown. Allow to cool in pan before removing, then put upside down on rack. (Makes 12 large muffins)

COCONUT MUFFINS

Delicate and delectable—not too sweet.

3 tablespoons margarine
¼ cup sugar
1 egg, beaten
3 tablespoons milk
½ cup + 2 tablespoons flour

¼ teaspoon salt
1 teaspoon baking powder
½ cup unsweetened
  coconut meal

Cream margarine and sugar; beat in egg and milk until smooth with wire whisk. In another bowl combine dry ingredients; beat into creamed mixture just until well combined. Bake in greased tiny muffin tins at 400° about 15 minutes, until golden. (Makes 16 mini muffins)

WALNUT MUFFINS

¾ cup flour
½ teaspoon baking powder
½ teaspoon soda
¾ teaspoon salt
1 tablespoon sugar

1 egg, beaten
2 tablespoons milk
2 tablespoons dairy sour
  cream
¼ cup margarine, melted
⅓ cup chopped walnuts

Mix dry ingredients together. Beat egg; add milk, sour cream, and melted margarine; beat until smooth with wire whisk. Stir into dry mixture just until well combined; fold in nuts. Bake in greased muffin tins at 400° about 15 minutes. (Makes 6 large muffins or 14 mini muffins)

BANANA MUFFINS

6 tablespoons margarine
¼ cup granulated sugar
¼ cup brown sugar
1 egg
2 tablespoons lemon juice

1½ cups mashed ripe banana
1¼ cups flour
¼ teaspoon salt
¾ teaspoon baking soda
1 teaspoon baking powder

Cream margarine and sugars together in large bowl; add next 3 ingredients and beat well. In another bowl mix dry ingredients; beat into banana mixture just until well combined. Bake in greased muffin tins at 375° about 25 minutes, or until browned. (Makes 12 mini muffins plus 7 regular-sized ones)

BREADS

CORN MUFFINS ESPAGNOLE

2 tablespoons margarine
⅓ cup finely chopped onion
¼ cup milk
¼ cup grated sharp cheese
¼ cup finely diced green
  pepper
¼ cup finely chopped
  pimiento-stuffed olives

1 egg, beaten
½ cup flour
⅔ cup corn meal
2 teaspoons baking powder
¼ teaspoon seasoned salt
⅛ teaspoon Lawry's
  garlic salt

Melt margarine in skillet and sauté onion till limp. Stir in milk, cheese, green pepper, olives, and lastly, beaten egg. In mixing bowl combine dry ingredients; beat into onion mixture just until well combined. Fill greased muffin pans full and bake at 400° for about 20 minutes, until browned. (Makes 20 mini muffins)

CRESCENT ROLLS

Refrigerated crescent rolls are so easy to convert into all sorts of tasty treats. Spread the dough with the filling of your choice before rolling up and baking. Make them either regulation size (for big appetites), or cut in half for "mini buns." Here are some suggestions for fillings: bacon and cheese; minced sautéed mushrooms; chopped olives; toasted sesame seeds.

TINY BAKED MUSHROOM SANDWICHES

6 slices bread
2 tablespoons soft butter
¼ cup dairy sour cream

2 tablespoons beef flavor
  mushroom soup mix

Trim bread. Combine sour cream and soup mix and spread on 3 slices bread. Top with the other 3 slices. Spread tops and bottoms of sandwiches with soft butter. Cut each sandwich into fourths. Bake at 375° about 15 minutes, or until browned. (Makes 12 tiny square sandwiches, serving 4)

TOASTED ONION SANDWICH FINGERS

4 teaspoons onion soup mix　　　Butter (or margarine)
⅓ cup dairy sour cream
6 slices thin-sliced bread

Combine soup mix and sour cream. Cut each slice of bread into 3 strips. Match up strips to make 9 sandwiches. Spread bottom strips with butter and arrange on cookie sheet, butter side down. Spread top slices with the onion mixture and put on top to make sandwiches. Bake at 350° until well browned. (Makes 9 finger sandwiches)

MINI BUNS

1 package (8 oz.) refrigerated　　Melted butter
　crescent rolls

Roll out dough and divide into 2 sections. Ignore the diagonal perforations. Cut each section into 4 thin rectangles, making 16 strips. Roll each strip up like a jelly roll and fit into tiny muffin cups (greased, if not Teflon). Brush with melted butter. Bake at 375° about 10 minutes.

These can be made ahead of time. Put muffin tins with rolled-up dough in refrigerator until ready to bake. (Makes 16 mini buns)

VEGETABLE MEDLEY

4 teaspoons margarine
1 cup chopped onion
1 clove garlic, smashed
1 can (8 oz.) tomato sauce
2 tomatoes (fresh or canned), cut up and drained
2 tablespoons minced pimiento
1½ cups diced summer squash
1 cup chopped green pepper
16 pimiento-stuffed olives, quartered
½ teaspoon garlic salt
Dash oregano (or Italian seasoning)

Melt margarine in skillet; sauté onion and garlic until tender. Stir in tomato sauce, then remaining ingredients, except squash. Cook squash in small amount of water until barely tender; drain. Mix with other vegetables. Bake in casserole at 350° about 45 minutes. (Serves 8)

PINEAPPLE WINE CARROTS

8 medium large carrots
3 tablespoons cornstarch
¼ cup cold water
2 tablespoons lemon juice
½ cup frozen pineapple juice concentrate
2 tablespoons butter
½ teaspoon salt
¼ cup pineapple wine

Cut scraped carrots into slivers, then cut in half. Cook in small amount of water until tender; drain. Mix cornstarch with water, lemon juice, and pineapple juice; cook until thick and clear, stirring; add carrots. Just before serving, while still hot, stir in butter and salt, then wine. (Serves 8)

CURAÇAO CARROTS

8 medium-sized carrots
2 tablespoons cornstarch
⅓ cup cold water
2 tablespoons lemon juice
½ cup frozen orange juice concentrate
2 tablespoons butter
½ teaspoon salt
½ cup curaçao

Scrape carrots and cut in thin slivers. Cook in small amount of water until tender; drain. Mix cornstarch, water, and fruit juices; cook until thick and clear. Add to cooked carrots. When ready to serve, stir in butter, salt, and curaçao. Heat, but do not boil. (Serves 8)

TIPSY BANANA CARROTS

8 medium-sized carrots
1 tablespoon cornstarch
¼ cup lemon juice
¼ cup cold water
1 tablespoon sugar

1 cup mashed ripe bananas
½ teaspoon salt
4 teaspoons butter
½ cup banana liqueur
(Leroux brand recommended)

Cut scraped carrots into slivers, then cut in half. Cook in small amount of water until tender; drain. Mix cornstarch with lemon juice and water; cook until thick and clear. Add sugar and mashed banana; cook 3 minutes. Add cooked carrots. Just before serving, stir in salt, butter, and liqueur. (Serves 8)

TAHITIAN SPINACH

⅔ cup unsweetened coconut meal*
1¼ teaspoons hickory smoked salt

⅔ cup dairy sour cream
2 packages frozen chopped spinach

* sold in health food stores

Stir together coconut meal and smoked salt until well mixed; combine with sour cream. Refrigerate, covered, until ready to serve. Cook spinach in small amount of water; drain. When ready to serve stir in reserved coconut mixture. (Serves 8)

VEGETABLES

SHERRY BAKED ONIONS

12 medium onions, sliced
½ teaspoon salt
1 egg yolk

½ cup sweetened condensed
milk
¾ cup cream sherry

Cook sliced onions in small amount of water until soft; drain. Put in greased casserole and sprinkle with salt. Stir together egg yolk, condensed milk, and sherry; pour over onions. Bake at 325° for 15 minutes. (Serves 8)

ORIENTAL GREEN BEANS

1 cup sliced mushrooms
1 tablespoon butter
1 cup thinly sliced celery
2 packages frozen Italian
  green beans
  (or 4 cups cut-up fresh
  green beans)

½ cup thinly sliced water
  chestnuts
1 teaspoon Lawry's garlic
  salt
Dash ground pepper
2 tablespoons butter

Sauté mushrooms in 1 tablespoon butter; set aside. Cook celery in small amount of water until almost tender (do not overcook). Remove from water and set aside in bowl. In same cooking water cook beans until barely tender; drain if necessary. When ready to serve, combine mushrooms and vegetables in saucepan and add chestnuts and seasonings. Heat well, then stir in butter. (Serves 8)

SAVORY BAKED POTATOES

4 large Idaho potatoes
3 tablespoons butter
¾ cup dairy sour cream
¼ cup yogurt (optional)

4 teaspoons chopped capers
3 tablespoons chopped chives
1 teaspoon garlic salt
Dash ground pepper

Grease potato skins. Bake at 400° about 1 hour. Cut in half lengthwise and scoop out insides, leaving skin intact. Mash scooped-out potato with remaining ingredients; refill skins with this mixture. Warm in oven a few minutes before serving. (Serves 8)

MUSHROOM SPINACH BAKE

1½ packages frozen chopped spinach
¾ cup dairy sour cream
1½ tablespoons lemon juice
1 envelope Lipton's beef flavor mushroom soup mix

Thaw spinach, but do not drain. Mix with remaining ingredients. Bake in greased casserole at 325° about 30 minutes. (Serves 8)

EGGPLANT CASSEROLE

4 slices dry bread
2 tablespoons butter, mashed with garlic
2 small eggplants, unpeeled and cubed
¼ cup minced onion
1 cup tomato catsup
1 can (1 lb.) peeled tomatoes, undrained
12 pimiento-stuffed olives, cut up
1½ cups grated sharp cheese

Spread bread with the garlic butter. Cut into small pieces, and put in bottom of greased casserole. Add diced eggplant and minced onion; spread catsup evenly over top, then add tomatoes. Bake, covered, about 1 hour at 350°; then add olives and sprinkle with cheese. Bake, uncovered, ½ hour longer. (Serves 8)

ZUCCHINI MAJORCA

1 tablespoon olive oil
1 tablespoon butter
1½ cups chopped onion
1 clove garlic, cut up
2 cups diced zucchini
1 cup diced green pepper

½ cup diced celery
1 6-oz. can tomato paste
1 cup canned tomatoes (plus some liquid)
1½ teaspoons garlic salt
¾ teaspoon oregano

Heat oil and butter in large skillet; sauté onion and garlic, discarding garlic when it starts to color. Transfer to large casserole; add remaining ingredients and mix well. Bake at 350° for 1 hour, uncovered; then cover and bake at least ½ hour longer. (Serves 8-10)

GUAVA SWEET POTATOES

2½ cups cooked mashed sweet potatoes (or yams)
3 tablespoons butter

½ teaspoon salt
6 tablespoons guava jelly
3 tablespoons lemon juice

Mix ingredients. Heat well in saucepan, or bake in a greased casserole at 350° about 20 minutes. (Serves 8) NOTE: Do not use canned yams, since they are packed in heavy syrup and will be too sweet with the guava jelly added.

BANANA PEAS

2 packages frozen peas
2¼ cups mashed ripe banana

4 teaspoons butter
1 teaspoon salt

Cook peas in small amount of water until tender. Meanwhile, cooked mashed banana about 5 minutes. Drain peas, and add to cooked bananas with butter and salt. Heat thoroughly, mashing with potato masher. (Serves 8-10)

GRAPEFRUIT SPINACH SALAD

Grapefruit sections
Frozen chopped spinach

Lettuce
LEMON FRENCH DRESSING

Arrange grapefruit sections on lettuce. With a sharp knife shave off slices from a block of still-frozen spinach. Scatter over grapefruit. Serve with LEMON FRENCH DRESSING.

ITALIAN GREEN BEAN SALAD

1 package frozen Italian
   green beans
¼ cup vinegar
2 tablespoons olive oil
2 tablespoons safflower oil
2 tablespoons water
2 cloves garlic, cut in halves

1 tablespoon Italian
   dressing mix
½ cup chopped celery
2 artichoke hearts, cut up
1 tablespoon capers (or
   anchovies)
Lettuce

The day before, cook beans in small amount of water and drain; cut beans in squares. Combine next 6 ingredients; add cooked beans. Refrigerate in covered container several hours or overnight. When ready to serve, discard garlic, and add celery and capers. Serve on lettuce. (Serves 4)

GRAPEFRUIT AVOCADO SALAD

Grapefruit sections   Lettuce
Avocado slices   LEMON FRENCH DRESSING

Combine grapefruit and avocado slices on lettuce leaves. Dip avocado slices in lemon juice to prevent discoloring, or soak them in the dressing until serving time.

GRAPEFRUIT ZUCCHINI SALAD

Grapefruit sections   Lettuce
Grated raw zucchini   LEMON FRENCH DRESSING

Arrange lettuce on plates, and cover with grapefruit sections. Grate the zucchini over this arrangement with a Mouli grater, or another type of coarse grater, using largest holes. Serve with LEMON FRENCH DRESSING.

TOMATO CHEESE SALAD

6 oz. natural Swiss cheese,   1 teaspoon grated onion
    cut in strips   ½ teaspoon paprika
2 hard-cooked eggs, diced   4 pimiento-stuffed olives,
¼ cup diced celery   sliced
1¼ cups dairy sour cream   2 large tomatoes, sliced
¼ cup yogurt   Lettuce
¼ teaspoon garlic salt

Combine first 9 ingredients. Chill until ready to serve. Arrange tomato slices on lettuce leaves; cover with chilled cheese mixture. (Serves 4)

FRUIT AND VEGETABLE SALAD

Grapefruit sections
Orange sections
Avocado slices
½ cup raw peas, grated
1 small raw zucchini,
   grated
Lettuce and watercress

DRESSING:
¼ cup safflower oil
¼ cup lemon juice
½ teaspoon paprika
½ teaspoon salt
¼ teaspoon dry mustard

Arrange fruit artistically on greens; sprinkle with grated vegetables. Pour the dressing. (Serves 4).

GREEN BALL SALAD

Honeydew melon balls
Tiny avocado balls
Tiny zucchini balls
   (optional)
Raw peas
Round seedless green grapes

Lettuce
Watercress
Minted cream cheese balls
   (optional)
FLUFFY GREEN DRESSING

Garnish each serving (if desired) with 1 or 2 cream cheese balls, which have been stuffed with a piece of water chestnut and rolled in finely snipped fresh mint leaves.

ARTICHOKE CELERY SALAD

1 garlic clove
2 tablespoons safflower oil
1 tablespoon olive oil
1 tablespoon wine vinegar
1 tablespoon lemon juice
½ teaspoon paprika
½ teaspoon seasoned salt

1 teaspoon chopped chives
2 canned artichoke hearts
  cut in quarters
½ cup diced celery
4 pimiento-stuffed
  olives, cut up
Salad greens

Make the dressing the night before. Slash garlic clove in several places, but not all the way through; add it to the next 6 ingredients. Refrigerate in tightly covered container all night. Next day just before serving, remove garlic; mix in chives, artichoke pieces, celery, and olives. Serve on greens. Garnish with cherry tomatoes, if desired. (Serves 4)

ARTICHOKE TOMATO SALAD

Make according to artichoke celery salad, but add 2 cut-up peeled tomatoes instead of the celery and olives.

MIXED VEGETABLE SALAD

Cherry tomatoes, halved
Diced celery
Grated raw zucchini
Raw peas (or frozen)

Avocado slices (optional)
Lettuce
Watercress
LEMON FRENCH DRESSING

Arrange vegetables on 4 salad plates. Vary the amounts as you desire. Garnish with lettuce and watercress. Pass the dressing.

RAW VEGETABLE SALAD

Shredded lettuce
4 artichoke hearts,
   cut up
½ cup chopped celery
2 sliced green onions

¼ cup grated raw peas
¾ cup grated zucchini
LEMON FRENCH DRESSING
   (or Roquefort)

Arrange lettuce on salad plates; cover with layers of the vegetables in order given. Dribble with dressing. (Serves 4)

GRAPEFRUIT VEGETABLE SALAD

Grapefruit sections
½ cup chopped celery
½ cup raw peas, grated

1 cup grated raw zucchini
Lettuce
LEMON FRENCH DRESSING

Arrange lettuce on plates; cover with grapefruit sections and celery. Sprinkle grated vegetables on top, and dribble with dressing. (Serves 4)

MOLDED VEGETABLE SALADS

GREEN VEGETABLE MOLD

½ package frozen green
  beans, cooked
½ cup frozen peas, *not* cooked
2 green onions and 1 inch
  of their stems
¼ cup diced avocado
2 teaspoons gelatin
⅓ cup water

2 tablespoons lemon juice
1 tablespoon salad oil
¼ teaspoon seasoned salt
Dash garlic salt
¼ teaspoon paprika
2 tablespoons yogurt
Watercress

Cook beans in small amount of water until tender. Put in blender with ½ cup cooking water; add minced onions, avocado, and the uncooked peas. Combine lemon juice, oil, and seasonings; add to vegetables. Soften gelatin in the ⅓ cup water 5 minutes, then dissolve, stirring over low heat; add to vegetables in blender with yogurt. Run until smooth. Chill in 4 individual oiled molds. Serve with watercress, and pass your favorite French dressing. (Serves 4)

CURRIED AVOCADO MOLD

2 teaspoons gelatin
½ cup water
3 tablespoons lemon juice
1 cup mashed avocado
1 teaspoon grated onion
1 hard-cooked egg, cut up

2 tablespoons dairy sour
  cream
1 tablespoon salad oil
½ teaspoon salt
½ teaspoon curry powder
Cherry tomatoes

Soften gelatin in the water; dissolve, stirring over low heat. Remove from heat and add remaining ingredients; run in blender until smooth. Chill in 4 oiled molds until firm. Unmold on salad greens. Serve with LEMON FRENCH DRESSING. Garnish with cherry tomatoes. (Serves 4)

MOLDED SPINACH SALAD

A symphony in greens! The bright green peas stud the dark green mounds like jewels—all nestled under a cloud of pale green.

¼ package frozen chopped spinach*	½ cup chopped raw peas
¾ cup water	¼ cup chopped celery
2 teaspoons gelatin	Lettuce
½ cup water	Watercress
4 teaspoons lemon juice	Cherry tomatoes
4 teaspoons safflower oil	(optional)
¾ teaspoon onion salt	FLUFFY GREEN DRESSING

*Use fresh spinach if you prefer.

Cook spinach in ¾ cup water briefly. Pour into measuring cup with cooking water; add water to measure ¾ cup. Soften gelatin in ½ cup water 5 minutes; stir over low heat until dissolved. Stir in spinach, lemon juice, onion salt, peas, and celery. Chill in 4 individual oiled molds until firm. Unmold on salad plates and surround with greens. Garnish with halved cherry tomatoes, if desired. Serve with FLUFFY GREEN DRESSING. (Serves 4)

TOMATO CRANBERRY ASPIC

2 teaspoons gelatin   ½ cup whole raw cranberries
¾ cup tomato juice

Soften gelatin in about half of the tomato juice 5 minutes. Stir over low heat until dissolved. Run remaining juice and the cranberries in blender until smooth. Gradually stir into warm gelatin mixture. Chill in 4 individual oiled molds. Serve with lettuce or watercress. (Serves 4)

ASPARAGUS ARTICHOKE MOLD

1 cup cut-up asparagus   3 tablespoons minced celery
1 cup water   3 tablespoons minced green
2 tablespoons vinegar   pepper
1 tablespoon lemon juice   ¼ cup grated raw zucchini
1 tablespoon safflower oil   ½ teaspoon onion salt
1 tablespoon olive oil   ½ teaspoon garlic salt
2 artichoke hearts, cut   ⅛ teaspoon oregano
   in small pieces   ¼ teaspoon dry mustard

Cook asparagus in the 1 cup water till barely tender, then cut up and measure 1 cup. Run in blender with ½ cup of the cooking water, the vinegar, lemon juice, and oils. Put remaining ½ cup asparagus water in saucepan; sprinkle the gelatin over it. Dissolve, stirring over low heat. Cool at room temperature while cutting up the vegetables, which are then added. Stir in seasonings and puréed asparagus. Chill in 4 individual oiled molds till firm. Unmold on salad plates, surround with shredded lettuce and serve with FLUFFY GREEN DRESSING. Garnish with a cherry tomato, if desired. (Serves 4)

TOMATO ARTICHOKE ASPIC

1 envelope plain gelatin
¾ cup cold water
¼ cup lemon juice
1 can (8 oz.) tomato sauce

½ cup chopped celery
½ cup cut-up canned artichoke hearts, drained
2 teaspoons cut-up capers

Put water in saucepan; sprinkle gelatin on top. Stir till dissolved over low heat. Stir in lemon juice and tomato sauce. Cool a bit, then add vegetables. Divide into 4 oiled molds and chill until firm. Unmold and serve with greens and YOGURT MAYONNAISE. (Serves 4)

JELLIED GAZPACHO

Spanish gazpacho almost always includes cucumber, but since many people dislike it, I recommend serving the cucumber separately (chopped up) in a small bowl for those who do like it. Even in Spain I found that in some restaurants they serve it this way.

1 envelope gelatin
1½ cups tomato juice
2 tablespoons vinegar
1 teaspoon garlic salt
1 teaspoon paprika
¼ cup sliced green onions

¼ cup finely chopped celery
½ cup finely chopped green pepper
1 large tomato, peeled and chopped

Soften gelatin in ¼ cup tomato juice. Heat remaining juice; add softened gelatin and stir over low heat until dissolved. Add remaining ingredients. Chill in 4 oiled individual molds until firm. Serve on greens with salad dressing. (Serves 4)

FRUIT SALADS

GREEN AND WHITE FRUIT SALAD

Diced fresh pineapple
Diced fresh pears
Grapefruit sections
Honeydew melon balls

Seedless green grapes
Cottage cheese
Lettuce and watercress
LEMON FRENCH DRESSING

EARLY OCTOBER FRUIT SALAD

Fresh cranberries,
  cut up
Fresh blueberries
Diced fresh pineapple
Diced fresh pears

Cottage cheese
Lettuce
Watercress
LEMON FRENCH DRESSING

FROZEN FRUIT SALAD

½ cup cottage cheese
¼ cup dairy sour cream
2 tablespoons lemon juice
½ cup crushed pineapple
¼ cup diced pears
⅓ cup sliced strawberries

¼ cup blueberries
1 tablespoon sugar
¾ cup whipped topping
Lettuce and watercress
FLUFFY GREEN DRESSING

Mash cottage cheese with sour cream and lemon juice with a fork until smooth. Mix in fruit and sugar, then fold in whipped topping. Freeze in foil-lined ice cube tray until firm. Thaw 20-30 minutes before serving in squares on the greens. Pass GREEN DRESSING. (If frozen strawberries are used, omit sugar, since they are sweetened.) (Serves 4)

GUAVA SALAD

1 envelope gelatin
1½ cups guava nectar
2 tablespoons lemon juice

¼ cup diced pineapple
Lettuce
EIDERDOWN DRESSING

Soak gelatin in ½ cup of the nectar 5 minutes, then dissolve over low heat. Stir in remaining nectar and the lemon juice. Chill until syrupy, then add pineapple. Chill in molds until firm. Serve with EIDERDOWN DRESSING on lettuce. (Serves 4)

GOLDEN FRUIT SALAD

2 teaspoons gelatin
¾ cup water
⅛ teaspoon salt
½ teaspoon paprika
¼ teaspoon dry mustard
2 tablespoons lemon juice
⅓ cup frozen orange juice
    concentrate

1 cup drained orange sections
    cut in small pieces
½ cup coarsely grated
    carrots
Salad greens
EIDERDOWN DRESSING

Soften gelatin in the water 5 minutes. Stir over low heat with salt, paprika, and mustard until dissolved. Add fruit juices while stirring; chill until syrupy, then fold in orange pieces and grated carrots. Chill in 4 individual oiled molds until firm. Unmold on salad greens and serve with EIDERDOWN DRESSING. Garnish with mandarin orange sections if desired. (Serves 4)

FRUIT SALADS

WINTER SALAD

Raw cranberries
Grapefruit sections
Diced apples

Halved and seeded green
grapes
Grated carrot (optional)

Serve on lettuce with LEMON FRENCH DRESSING. The grapes and cranberries may be frozen ahead of time and will keep indefinitely.

ORANGE GRAPEFRUIT SALAD

2 grapefruits
½ cup orange segments
1 large carrot, grated
¼ cup frozen orange
juice concentrate
1 tablespoon grated orange
rind
¼ cup lemon juice

¼ cup safflower oil
¼ cup yogurt
2 tablespoons dairy sour
cream
½ teaspoon salt
½ teaspoon dry mustard
2 tablespoons toasted almonds
Lettuce

Dig out grapefruit pulp with pointed spoon; arrange on lettuce with orange segments. Sprinkle with grated carrot. Make a dressing out of the next 8 ingredients; spoon over salad; garnish with almonds. (Serves 4)

FLORIDA SALAD

Grapefruit sections
Diced avocado
Sliced water chestnuts

Slivered pimiento
Lettuce and watercress
LEMON FRENCH DRESSING

110

AVOCADO FRUIT NUT SALAD

Sliced avocado
Grapefruit sections
Fresh pineapple chunks
Chopped cashew nuts
Salad greens
FLUFFY GREEN DRESSING

TROPICAL FRUIT SALAD

Fresh pineapple, diced
Fresh papaya (or other melon)
  peeled and diced
Fresh pears, diced
Fresh mangoes, peeled and
  diced
Canned guava shells, diced
Ripe bananas, sliced
Fresh strawberries,
  halved
Kiwi fruit, peeled and
  sliced
Cottage cheese
Toasted almonds (optional)
Lettuce
PINEAPPLE DRESSING

Use any or all of these fruits. Arrange on lettuce. Top each serving with a ball of cottage cheese. Sprinkle with almonds, if desired. Pass PINEAPPLE DRESSING in a small bowl.

FRUIT AVOCADO DESSERT SALAD

4 canned Bartlett pear
  halves
½ can grapefruit sections
½ cup canned pineapple
  tidbits
½ peeled avocado, sliced
4 scoops cottage cheese
Lettuce
Watercress
AVOCADO PINEAPPLE
  DRESSING

On 4 salad dishes put 1 pear half in center; surround with remaining fruit. Put a scoop of cottage cheese in each pear cavity; cover with AVOCADO PINEAPPLE DRESSING. Surround with lettuce and watercress. (Serves 4)

111

MOLDED FRUIT SALADS

APRICOT CARROT SALAD MOLD

1 envelope gelatin
1 can (12 oz.) apricot
    nectar
4 teaspoons lemon juice
¼ cup canned pear juice
¾ cup diced canned pears

⅔ cup grated raw carrots
¼ cup diced celery
Lettuce and watercress
2 sliced frozen bananas
CREAMY PINEAPPLE
    DRESSING

Soften gelatin in the lemon juice and part of the apricot nectar 5 minutes, then dissolve, stirring over low heat. Add pear juice and remaining nectar. Cool slightly, then add pears and vegetables. Chill in 4 individual oiled molds until firm. Unmold and serve surrounded with greens and the sliced frozen bananas (or other fruit), and pass CREAMY PINEAPPLE DRESSING. (Serves 4)

STRAWBERRY SALAD MOLD

1 envelope gelatin
½ cup cold water
1 package (10 oz.) frozen
    sliced strawberries
1 package (3 oz.) cream
    cheese

½ cup dairy sour cream
½ cup canned crushed
    pineapple, undrained
1 very ripe banana, sliced
Salad greens

Soften gelatin in the water 5 minutes. Dissolve, stirring over low heat. Add frozen berries and stir just until separated. Mash cream cheese and sour cream with a fork; add to gelatin mixture. Stir in pineapple and fold in sliced banana. Chill in oiled molds. Serve with greens. (Serves 4)

112

FLUFFY GREEN MAYONNAISE

1 egg white, beaten stiff ¼ cup dairy sour cream
½ cup Hellman's mayonnaise 3 drops green food color
¼ cup yogurt

Combine last 4 ingredients with wire whisk; fold into beaten egg white. (Makes 1 ¼ cups)

CURRY AVOCADO DRESSING

½ cup mashed avocado ¼ teaspoon curry powder
½ cup yogurt   ¼ teaspoon onion salt
3 tablespoons lemon juice Dash garlic powder

Run in blender. Serve with seafood, or as a dip. (Makes 1 cup)

AVOCADO GREEN DRESSING

6 tablespoons safflower oil Dash of salt
6 tablespoons lemon juice 2 tablespoons mashed
6 tablespoons dairy sour avocado (or ½ drop
 cream   green coloring)

If avocado is used to tint the salad green, run it with oil and lemon juice in blender, then mix in sour cream and salt. If bottled coloring is used, dilute with a little water to get a pale tint of green, since too strong a color is unattractive. If desired, run a few watercress leaves in blender with the dressing for more green effect. (Makes about 1 cup)

SALAD DRESSINGS

AVOCADO PINEAPPLE DRESSING

Thick, smooth, and a lovely green color. Ideal on a grape-fruit or avocado salad.

¼ cup mashed avocado
¼ cup lemon juice
1 tablespoon safflower oil
2 tablespoons dairy sour
  cream

¼ cup yogurt
Dash of salt
2 tablespoons frozen pineapple juice, undiluted

Run all ingredients in blender. (Makes about ⅔ cup dressing, serving 4)

CREAMY PINEAPPLE DRESSING

2 tablespoons mayonnaise
2 tablespoons lemon juice
1 tablespoon frozen pineapple
  juice concentrate

⅓ cup frozen whipped
  topping, thawed
1 drop green coloring
  (optional)

Mix well with wire whisk. Refrigerate in covered container until ready to use. (Makes about ½ cup dressing—enough for 4 fruit salads)

EIDERDOWN DRESSING

¼ cup yogurt
2 tablespoons dairy sour
  cream
1 tablespoon safflower oil

1 tablespoon lemon juice
⅛ teaspoon salt
1 egg white, beaten stiff

Combine first 5 ingredients, beating until smooth with wire whisk. Fold in beaten egg white. This can be made the day before and will keep 2 or 3 days if tightly covered. (Makes ½ cup dressing, serving 4)

FLUFFY GREEN DRESSING

Add 1 drop green food color to EIDERDOWN DRESSING.

PINEAPPLE DRESSING

½ cup yogurt
¼ cup dairy sour cream
¼ cup lemon juice
2 tablespoons safflower oil

2 tablespoons frozen pineapple juice, undiluted
Dash of salt

Beat together with wire whisk. (Serves 4)

YOGURT MAYONNAISE

¼ cup Hellman's mayonnaise
2 tablespoons yogurt
2 tablespoons lemon juice

Dash garlic salt (or
plain salt)

Mix well. (Serves 4)

LEMON FRENCH DRESSING

⅓ cup lemon juice
⅓ cup safflower oil
½ teaspoon paprika

Dash garlic salt (only
for vegetable
salads)

Mix well. (Serves 4)

115

FROZEN DESSERTS

FROZEN PEAR HELENE

12 canned Bartlett pear
halves, diced
1 cup frozen whipped topping,
thawed

¼ cup white crème de
cacao
½ cup raspberry syrup
(bottled)

Freeze pears. Put in dessert dishes and cover with a dollop of the topping mixed with the liqueur. Pour over raspberry syrup. (Serves 4)

NECTARINE SHERBET

1 cup yogurt
1½ cups chopped, unpeeled
nectarines

⅓ cup sugar
3 tablespoons crème de
almond

Run in blender until smooth. Freeze in covered container until mushy. If too hard, let it thaw a bit before serving. (Serves 4)

ORANGE BANANA SHERBET

1 cup mashed ripe banana
½ cup water
¼ cup frozen orange juice
concentrate

3 tablespoons curaçao
(or Cointreau)

Cook mashed banana about three minutes, then put in blender with remaining ingredients; run until smooth. Freeze in covered container. Allow to thaw a few minutes before serving. (Serves 4)

STRAWBERRY SHERBET

1 pint strawberries, ¼ cup sugar
  cut up ¾ cup yogurt
2 tablespoons lemon juice

Run in blender until smooth. Freeze until mushy. If too hard, allow to thaw a bit before serving. (If frozen berries are used, add much less sugar, since they are already sweetened.) (Serves 4)

GRAND MARNIER ICE CREAM

This has a delicious orange brandy flavor. Most unusual and sophisticated.

1 pint vanilla ice cream 3 tablespoons Grand Marnier
  liqueur

Soften ice cream in refrigerator until right consistency to stir. Mix in liqueur. Freeze several hours in covered container. (Serves 4)

GREEN SURPRISE ICE CREAM

1 pint vanilla ice cream 2 tablespoons white crème de
¼ cup blue curaçao cacao

Mix ingredients. Freeze in covered container several hours or overnight. (Serves 4)

PINK PANTHER PARFAIT

Very attractive with its pink fluff topping. It separates into 2 layers, the lighter one at top.

1 envelope gelatin
1½ cups bottled cranberry juice cocktail

1 cup vanilla ice cream
¼ cup crème de almond liqueur

Soften gelatin in the cranberry juice; stir over low heat until dissolved. Add ice cream by spoonfuls, stirring until melted after each addition. Chill in 4 parfait glasses. When firm, cover with ¾ cup whipped topping mixed with the crème de almond. (Serves 4)

PINK PEPPERMINT SUNDAE

¾ cup bottled cranberry juice cocktail
4 teaspoons cornstarch
2 tablespoons sugar

2 tablespoons peppermint schnapps
1 pint vanilla ice cream

Cook cranberry juice and cornstarch until thick and clear; add sugar and cook about 1 minute. Stir in the peppermint liqueur. Serve hot or cold over ice cream.(Serves 4)

COFFEE CRUNCH ICE CREAM

1 pint vanilla ice cream
2 teaspoons instant coffee
1 cup crumbled coffee cookies

¼ cup vodka
3 tablespoons crème de cacao

Mix well and freeze. (Serves 4)

RASPBERRY SHERRY MOUSSE

A pretty pink concoction with irresistible flavor.

2 jars (4½ oz. each) baby food raspberry cobbler

½ cup frozen whipped topping, thawed
3 tablespoons cream sherry

Mix well and freeze. (Serves 4)

JUNE FRUIT SHERBET

2 cups diced fresh rhubarb
½ cup water
4 teaspoons honey
1 cup diced fresh pineapple

½ cup sliced fresh strawberries
1 egg white

Simmer rhubarb in the water with honey until soft, but not mushy. Run in blender with pineapple and strawberries until smooth. Beat egg white until stiff and fold in fruit purée. Freeze until mushy. Serve in sherbet glasses. (Serves 4)

ROYAL PURPLE ICE CREAM

Who said you couldn't whip up a company dessert in 5 minutes?

2 cups dairy sour cream
1⅓ cups frozen grape juice concentrate

Mix well and freeze. (Serves 4)

GRAPE PEAR SHERBET

1 can (1 lb.) pears
3 tablespoons frozen grape
  juice, undiluted

½ cup milk
3 tablespoons white
  crème de cacao

Cut up pears; dump into blender with syrup from can and remaining ingredients. Run until smooth. Freeze in covered container. (Serves 4)

LEMON AVOCADO SHERBET

¼ cup mashed avocado
⅛ teaspoon salt
¾ cup sugar
½ cup lemon juice

1 teaspoon grated lemon rind
1 pint milk
4 avocado halves

Combine first five ingredients; add to milk. Freeze. Serve in unpeeled avocado halves. (Serves 4)

MANGO ICE CREAM

This is a magical combination! It tastes like mango, but the orange liqueur enhances the flavor.

1 pint vanilla ice cream
1 cup mango pulp

3 tablespoons Grand Marnier

Mix and freeze in covered container. (Serves 4)

CASHEW BRITTLE ICE CREAM

¼ cup cashew nut brittle, ground in meat grinder

1 pint vanilla ice cream

Add the ground candy to the softened ice cream. Freeze to firmness. (Serves 4)

BLISSFUL DREAM ICE CREAM

1 pint vanilla ice cream
3 Heath candy bars, crushed
⅓ cup white crème de cacao

2 tablespoons chopped toasted almonds

Mix well and freeze several hours in covered container. (Serves 4)

FROZEN DESSERTS

COCONUT ALMOND ICE CREAM

1 pint vanilla ice cream
½ cup unsweetened coconut
 meal*

¼ cup chopped, toasted,
 salted almonds

* available at health food stores

Mix and freeze in covered container. (Serves 4)

MACAROON ICE CREAM

8 macaroons
3 tablespoons crème de
 almond

1 pint vanilla ice
 cream

Roll dry macaroons into crumbs, add with the liqueur to slightly softened ice cream. Freeze in covered container. (Serves 4)

AVOCADO ICE CREAM

1 pint ice cream
 (vanilla)
1¼ cups mashed avocado

⅓ cup sugar
3 tablespoons lemon juice
½ teaspoon almond extract

Soften ice cream slightly and mix in remaining ingredients. Freeze until firm, but not hard. (Serves 4)

APRICOT SHERBET

14 dried apricots,
  cut up
1 cup water
2 teaspoons lemon juice

½ cup apricot preserves
½ cup yogurt

Cook apricots, covered, in the water until soft; drain juice into a measuring pitcher; add water to measure 1 cup. Add lemon juice, apricot preserves, and cooked apricots; cool slightly, then add yogurt. Whirl in blender until smooth. Freeze until mushy. (Serves 4)

BLUEBERRY GRAPE SHERRY ICE CREAM

1 pint vanilla ice cream
½ cup blueberry pie filling
¼ cup sherry
2 tablespoons frozen grape juice
  concentrate

3 tablespoons white
  crème de cacao

Soften ice cream slightly. Combine next 4 ingredients and run in blender until mixed. Stir into softened ice cream. Freeze in covered container. (Serves 4)

PEAR BAVARIAN

1½ cups pear nectar
1 envelope gelatin
3 tablespoons white crème
de cacao

¾ cup low-calorie
whipped topping
Crystallized violets

Soften gelatin in about ½ cup of the nectar, then dissolve over low heat. Very gradually stir in remaining nectar and the liqueur. Chill until thick; then beat in whipped topping. Chill in sherbet glasses several hours (overnight is best). Garnish with whipped topping and crystallized violets, if desired. (Serves 4)

DANISH PEAR MOLD

2 teaspoons gelatin
1⅓ cups syrup from can
of pears
½ cup milk

¼ cup raspberry syrup
2 tablespoons white crème
de cacao

Soften gelatin in the pear syrup 5 minutes, then dissolve over low heat. Stir in remaining ingredients. Chill in molds. Serve garnished with a bit of whipped topping. (Serves 4)

GRAPE BAVARIAN

1 tablespoon gelatin
¾ cup cold water
6 tablespoons frozen grape
juice concentrate

2 tablespoons lemon juice
¾ cup prepared low-
calorie whipped
topping

Soften gelatin in the water 5 minutes, then dissolve over low heat. Slowly add grape juice, stirring, then lemon juice. Chill until syrupy; then beat in whipped topping with wire whisk. Chill in 4 individual oiled molds (or sherbet glasses) until firm. (Serves 4)

PURPLE PINEAPPLE MOLD

A lovely lavender color, flecked with red. Delicious and refreshing.

2 teaspoons gelatin
½ cup cold water
1 cup crushed pineapple
½ cup raw cranberries
½ cup yogurt

Soften gelatin in the cold water 5 minutes, then dissolve over low heat; stir pineapple in slowly, then the yogurt. Dump into blender container, add cranberries, and run until smooth. Chill in molds until firm. (Serves 4)

RHUBARB ALMOND MOUSSE

2 cups diced rhubarb
½ cup water
¼ cup honey
2 teaspoons gelatin
3 tablespoons cold water
1 cup whipped topping
2 tablespoons crème de almond

Cook rhubarb in the ¼ cup water with honey until soft. Run in blender till smooth. Meanwhile soften gelatin in the 3 tablespoons water 5 minutes; dissolve over low heat. Add puréed rhubarb. Chill until set, then beat until frothy with electric beater. Fold in whipped topping and almond liqueur. Chill in 4 individual oiled molds. (Serves 4)

127

GELATIN DESSERTS

ORANGE WINE JELLY

1 envelope gelatin
1 cup cold water
½ cup orange wine
¼ cup frozen orange juice
   concentrate

2 tablespoons sugar
1 envelope whipped topping
⅓ cup milk
2 tablespoons Grand Marnier
   (or Cointreau)

Soften gelatin in the water, then stir over low heat to dissolve. Add wine, then the orange juice and sugar, stirring until dissolved. Chill in oiled molds until firm. Serve topped with Grand Marnier flavored whipped topping. (Follow package directions, but use only ⅓ cup milk; add the Grand Marnier and omit vanilla.) (Serves 4)

LEMON FLUFF

2 teaspoons gelatin
½ cup cold water
3 tablespoons sugar

¼ cup lemon juice
1 teaspoon grated lemon rind
Whipped dry milk*

Sprinkle gelatin on the water in saucepan. Stir over low heat until dissolved; stir in sugar, lemon juice, and grated rind. Chill until syrupy, then beat with wire whisk. Fold in whipped dry milk. Chill in dessert dishes or 4 individually oiled molds. (Serves 4)

* WHIPPED DRY MILK: Chill bowl and beater. Whip ¼ cup instant nonfat dry milk with ¼ cup ice water until soft peaks form; add 1 tablespoon lemon juice and beat until stiff. Fold in 2 tablespoons sugar.

PURPLE PARFAIT

A very pretty, "dressy" dessert.

2 teaspoons gelatin
¾ cup cold water
¼ cup frozen grape juice
  concentrate

Frozen whipped topping,
  thawed

Soften gelatin in the water 5 minutes; stir over low heat until dissolved. Gradually stir in the grape juice. Chill until syrupy, then beat till fluffy. Put a little in 4 parfait glasses. Cover with a layer of whipped topping, then with another layer of the grape fluff, and end with more topping. Chill at least 1 hour. Garnish with crystallized violets, if desired. (Serves 4)

GRAPE JUICE PEAR MOLD

1½ cups cut-up canned
  pears, drained
2 teaspoons gelatin
1 cup water
¼ cup pear juice

3 tablespoons frozen grape
  juice concentrate
2 tablespoons lemon juice
3 tablespoons white crème de
  cacao

Divide pear pieces in 4 individually oiled molds, or in dessert dishes (not oiled). Soften gelatin in the water 5 minutes, then stir over low heat to dissolve. Gradually stir in pear juice, grape juice, and lemon juice, then crème de cacao; pour over pears. Chill until firm. Garnish with about ¾ cup chocolate flavored whipped topping, to which you beat in 2 tablespoons white crème de cacao and 2 teaspoons grape juice (to make it a pretty lavender color). Garnish with candied violets, if desired. (Serves 4)

ALMOND BROILED GRAPEFRUIT

2 large grapefruits
4 teaspoons sugar
4 maraschino cherries

3 tablespoons crème de
  almond

Cut each grapefruit in half; remove seeds, and core out the centers. Sprinkle with sugar. Broil until browned, then remove from heat and dribble the almond liqueur on top. Fill each center with a maraschino cherry. Serve hot. (Serves 4)

AQUA FRUIT CUP

The combined blue curaçao and yogurt makes a beautiful aqua color. Tastes divine, too!

1 cup fresh diced pineapple
1 cup cut-up fresh pears
½ cup grapefruit segments
½ cup honeydew balls

½ cup yogurt
¼ cup blue curaçao
¼ cup white corn syrup

Put fruit in 4 sherbet glasses. Combine yogurt, curaçao, and corn syrup; pour over fruit. Serve very cold. (Serves 4)

TIPSY PEARS AND RASPBERRIES

6 canned Bartlett pear
  halves
¼ cup syrup from pears
6 tablespoons white crème
  de cacao

½ cup frozen rasp-
  berries

Cut pears in small pieces; mix with syrup and liqueur. Refrigerate in tightly covered container until serving time. Divide equally in four dessert dishes and put a portion of raspberries on each serving. (Serves 4)

GUAVA GRAPEFRUIT COUPE

½ can (9 oz.) guava shells
  in heavy syrup

1 cup grapefruit segments

Drain grapefruit segments if canned; mix with the cut-up guava shells and their syrup. Chill. Serve in sherbet glasses. (Serves 4)

RASPBERRY SHERRY BISQUE

Pink, soft, and seductive.

2 jars (4½ oz. each) baby
  food raspberry cobbler
3 tablespoons cream sherry

½ cup frozen whipped
  topping, thawed

Mix well. Chill in dessert dishes several hours. (Serves 4)

GINGER FRUIT CUP

½ cup diced honeydew melon
½ cup seedless green grapes,
  halved
1 cup drained diced canned
  pears
1 cup pineapple tidbits
  (unsweetened variety)

½ cup ginger brandy
2 tablespoons toasted
  sliced almonds
2 tablespoons finely
  chopped, crystal-
  lized ginger

Mix well. Chill several hours. Serve in sherbet glasses. (Serves 4)

PINEAPPLE WINE FRUIT CUP

Diced fresh pears
Sliced fresh strawberries
Grapefruit sections
Melon balls
Diced avocado (optional)

2 tablespoons frozen pineapple juice
¼ cup pineapple wine
  (Mardi Gras brand recommended)

Mix all ingredients and chill several hours. (The fruit should measure about 2½ cups.) (Serves 4)

TROPICAL RUM FRUIT CUP

1 cup diced fresh pineapple
1 cup diced fresh papaya
½ cup diced pears

2 tablespoons frozen
  pineapple juice
2 tablespoons dark rum

Chill the fruit in the rum in a covered container. When ready to serve, mix with the pineapple juice and serve in 4 sherbet glasses. (Serves 4)

ORANGE BANANA PUDDING

3 tablespoons sugar
1½ tablespoons lemon juice
¼ cup cornstarch
3 tablespoons frozen orange
   juice concentrate
2 egg yolks

1 cup hot water
½ cup mashed ripe
   banana
1½ teaspoons butter
3 tablespoons curaçao

In saucepan mix first five ingredients, then add hot water while stirring; add mashed banana. Cook until mixture gets thick, stirring occasionally. Remove from heat and stir in butter and curaçao. Pour into dessert dishes and cover tightly with saran wrap; chill several hours or overnight. Serve with whipped topping flavored with curaçao, if desired. (Serves 4)

PEACH ALMOND DREAM

4 ripe peaches, peeled and
   cut up
2 tablespoons crème de almond

½ cup prepared boxed
   whipped topping

Mix ingredients and chill in covered container until ready to serve. When making the whipped topping, substitute ½ teaspoon almond extract for the vanilla. Delicious with almond cookies! (Serves 4)

BANANA CRANBERRY CARDINAL

1 cup chopped fresh
  cranberries
½ cup mashed ripe
  banana

½ cup crushed pineapple
  (canned)

Run all ingredients in blender till puréed; transfer to saucepan and boil two minutes. Chill. Serve in sherbet glasses. If desired, garnish with a dollop of sour cream or whipped topping. (Serves 4)

COFFEE DREAM CREAM

½ package vanilla instant
  pudding. (¼ cup)
1 cup milk

3½ tablespoons coffee
  liqueur
1 cup frozen whipped
  topping, thawed

Mix together first 3 ingredients; beat with rotary beater 1 minute. Fold in whipped topping with wire whisk. Chill in dessert dishes. This dessert is also delicious frozen. (Serves 4)

CELESTIAL SHERRY CREAM

½ package (¼ cup) vanilla
  instant pudding
1 cup milk

3½ tablespoons sherry
1 cup frozen whipped
  topping, thawed

Beat together pudding mix and milk 1 minute with rotary beater; beat in sherry and fold in whipped topping with wire whisk. Chill in dessert dishes several hours. (Serves 4)

GRAPEFRUIT CHERRY FRUIT CUP

1 cup pitted tart red
  cherries
½ cup juice from cherries
Pulp from 1½ large grapefruits

¼ cup crème de almond

If cherries are fresh, cook until soft without sugar. Mix all ingredients. Chill in sherbet glasses. (Serves 4)

RUM CHIFFON

½ package (¼ cup) vanilla
  instant pudding
1 cup milk

3 tablespoons dark rum
1 cup frozen whipped
  topping, thawed

Mix together first 3 ingredients; beat with rotary beater 1 minute. Fold in whipped topping with wire whisk. Chill in dessert dishes. (Serves 4)

RASPBERRIES AND STRAWBERRIES IMPERIAL

A heavenly pink color to delight the eye! This can easily share honors with Strawberries Romanoff—yet is not the least bit rich, and much quicker to fix.

1¼ cups fresh raspberries
1¼ cups fresh strawberries,
  cut up

¾ cup frozen whipped
  topping, thawed
¼ cup white crème de cacao

Mix well and chill. (Serves 4)

MISCELLANEOUS DESSERTS

ZABAGLIONE WITH PEACHES

2 egg yolks
2 tablespoons sugar
3½ tablespoons Marsala wine

1⅓ cups sweetened sliced
    peaches (or other
    fresh fruit)

In top of double boiler beat egg yolks slightly with rotary beater or whisk. Gradually beat in sugar and wine. Place over boiling water and continue beating until fluffy and slightly thickened. Remove from heat at once. Ladle sauce over peach slices. Garnish with a dab of whipped topping, if desired. (Serves 4)

LEMON PUDDING

⅔ cup sugar
2 teaspoons grated lemon rind
6 tablespoons lemon juice
¼ cup cornstarch

1 egg york
1 cup hot water
2 teaspoons butter
Whipped topping

In saucepan mix first five ingredients, then slowly add hot water while stirring. Cook until very thick, then remove from heat and stir in butter. Pour into sherbet glasses and chill. Serve with whipped topping flavored with 1 teaspoon of lemon extract instead of vanilla. (Serves 4)

GREEN AND WHITE REFRESHER

Put grapefruit sections and lemon (or pineapple) sherbet in sherbet glasses; pour green crème de menthe over this arrangement.

CHOCOLATE COCONUT COOKIES

¼ cup margarine
¼ cup sugar
¾ cup sweetened condensed
  milk
1 teaspoon vanilla

½ oz. cooking chocolate,
  melted
1 cup soft bread crumbs
½ cup cracker crumbs
½ cup coconut

Cream margarine and sugar; add condensed milk and vanilla, then melted chocolate. Mix well. Stir in crumbs and coconut. Drop on greased cookie sheet; flatten down with wet fingers. Bake at 350° about 8 minutes. (Makes 24-28 cookies)

OATMEAL COOKIES

Everybody is wild about these, so they are worth taking the little extra time to make so many. They'll disappear, don't worry!

1 cup (2 sticks) margarine
¾ cup white sugar
¾ cup brown sugar, packed
1 egg, beaten
1 teaspoon vanilla
½ cup flour

1 cup whole wheat flour
1 teaspoon soda
1 teaspoon cinnamon
1½ cups oats
½ cup chopped almonds
  (unblanched)

Cream together margarine and sugars; add beaten egg and vanilla. Mix together flour, soda, and cinnamon, then add to sugar mixture. Add oats and nuts. Place walnut-sized lumps of dough on a greased cooked sheet; flatten down with fingers. Bake at 350° about 7 minutes, or until lightly browned around edges. (Makes about 6 dozen cookies)

ALMOND COOKIES

1½ cups unsifted flour
½ teaspoon soda
¼ teaspoon salt
¾ cup butter (or margarine)

¼ cup light brown sugar
1 cup white sugar
1 egg
1 tablespoon almond extract
Blanched almonds

In a bowl mix flour, soda, and salt; set aside. In another bowl cream butter with sugars; add egg and almond extract; beat in dry mixture. Pinch off lumps of dough as large as walnuts. Place 12 on a lightly greased cookie sheet; press down with heel of hand until very thin. Put an almond on top of each cookie. Bake at 350° about 10 minutes or until lightly browned. Repeat with remainder of dough. (Makes 4 dozen cookies)

CHOCOLATE NUT BARS

½ cup margarine (1 stick)
1⅓ cups light brown sugar
2 eggs
¾ teaspoon vanilla
¼ teaspoon salt
1½ teaspoons baking powder

1 cup flour
½ cup stone-ground whole wheat flour
⅓ cup quick oats
4 oz. chocolate morsels
⅔ cup chopped nuts

Cream margarine and sugar; add eggs one at a time, beating well after each. Mix in dry ingredients. Stir in chocolate morsels and nuts. Spread evenly in 2 square 8" x 8" greased pans. Bake at 350° about 20 minutes or until light brown. (Makes 24 bars)

PECAN CRISPIES

How can anything as devastatingly delicious as these cookies be so good for you? Four proteins—nuts, oats, whole wheat, and egg. Crumble them and mix with softened vanilla ice cream, then freeze, for a super "butter crunch" ice cream.

¼ cup margarine
¼ cup butter
1 cup dark brown
   sugar, packed
1 egg
½ teaspoon vanilla

½ cup wholewheat flour
½ teaspoon salt
½ teaspoon soda
1¼ cups quick oats
⅓ cup chopped pecans
   (or filberts)

Cream together shortening and sugar; beat in egg and vanilla. Combine dry ingredients; stir into creamed mixture and add nuts. Put walnut-sized lumps of dough on greased cookie sheets; flatten down. Bake at 350° about 8-10 minutes until brown around edges. (Makes 3 dozen cookies)

CHEWY CINNAMON COOKIES

¼ cup margarine
¼ cup light brown sugar
¾ cup sweetened condensed
   milk

⅓ cup quick oats
2 cups crushed cinnamon
   graham crackers

Start oven at 350°. Cream margarine and sugar; mix in condensed milk, oats and crumbs. Drop by spoonfuls on greased cookie sheet; flatten down with wet fingers. Bake at 350° about 8 minutes. (Makes about 26 cookies)

139

COOKIES

COFFEE COOKIES

3 tablespoons margarine
2 tablespoons powdered sugar
1 tablespoon granulated sugar
1½ teaspoons instant coffee

½ teaspoon vanilla
2 tablespoons dairy sour
  cream
¼ cup flour

Start oven at 350°. Cream margarine with the sugars and coffee powder until smooth. Blend in vanilla and sour cream; beat well. Add flour. Drop by spoonfuls on greased cookie sheet. Flatten down and shape in circles with a knife. Bake at 350° about 8 minutes. (Makes 12 cookies)

COFFEE MACAROONS

¼ cup margarine
¼ cup sugar
¾ cup sweetened
  condensed milk
1 teaspoon vanilla

4 teaspoons instant coffee
1 tablespoon hot water
2½ cups very soft bread
  crumbs

Cream margarine and sugar together; mix in condensed milk and vanilla. Dissolve coffee powder in the hot water; add to creamed mixture; stir in crumbs. Drop lumps about the size of large walnuts on greased cookie sheet. Bake at 350° about 7-8 minutes, or until very faintly browned at edges. Do not overbake—they should be chewy. (Makes 28 small macaroons)

LACE COOKIES

1 cup old-fashioned oats
¼ cup whole wheat flour
1 cup brown sugar

1 egg
⅓ cup melted margarine
½ teaspoon vanilla

Mix well. Drop far apart on greased cookie sheet. Bake at 350° about 10 minutes. Cool about 1 minute before removing from sheet. (Makes 18 cookies)

PECAN PIE COOKIES

¼ cup margarine
¼ cup dark brown sugar
¾ cup sweetened condensed
  milk
1 teaspoon vanilla

2 cups graham cracker
  crumbs
¼ cup quick oats
⅓ cup chopped pecans

Cream margarine and brown sugar together; stir in condensed milk and vanilla; mix until smooth. Add crumbs, oats, and nuts. Drop on greased cookie sheet; flatten down with wet fingers. Bake at 350° about 7-8 minutes. Remove immediately from pan. (Makes 24-28 cookies)

BEST EVER LEMON COOKIES

Real lemon flavor—as tantalizing as lemon pie.

¼ cup margarine
½ cup sugar
1 egg yolk
1 tablespoon lemon juice

Grated rind of 1 lemon
¾ cup flour

Cream margarine and sugar together; add egg yolk, lemon juice, and grated rind. Mix well, then add flour. Put small lumps on greased cookie sheet; flatten down thin. Bake at 350° about 10 minutes. (Makes 24 cookies)

ALMOND CRUMB COOKIES

¼ cup margarine
2 tablespoons light
  brown sugar
2 tablespoons white sugar
¾ cup sweetened con-
  densed milk

1½ teaspoons almond extract
1½ cups bread crumbs
⅓ cup coarse cracker crumbs
⅓ cup quick oats

Cream margarine and sugars together; stir in condensed milk and almond extract, then crumbs and oats. Drop by spoonfuls on greased cookie sheet; flatten down with wet fingers. Bake at 350° about 8 minutes, or until delicately browned. Remove from sheet immediately. (Makes 24 cookies)

CHEWY BREAD CRUMB MACAROONS

½ can Reese almond paste
  (4 oz.)
⅓ cup sugar

1 egg white (unbeaten)
⅔ cup dry bread crumbs

Cut up almond paste in small pieces into bowl. Add sugar and butter. Mix with wooden spoon or cut with pastry mixer. Add egg white, and mix with wooden spoon until smooth. Stir in crumbs. Form small patties on greased cookie sheet; flatten down with wet fingers. Bake at 325° about 7 or 8 minutes until just barely golden. (Makes 18 cookies)

ANISE CRUMB COOKIES

¼ cup margarine
2 tablespoons light
  brown sugar
2 tablespoons white sugar
¾ cup sweetened condensed
  milk

1 teaspoon anise extract
1½ cup bread crumbs
⅓ cup cracker crumbs
⅓ cup quick oats
2 tablespoons anise seeds

Cream margarine and sugars; stir in condensed milk and anise extract, then crumbs and oats. Drop by spoonfuls on greased cookie sheet; flatten with wet fingers. Sprinkle with anise seeds. Bake at 350° about 7 or 8 minutes. Remove from sheet immediately and turn over. (Makes 24 cookies)

CANDY COOKIE BARS

These are probably the most expensive and fattening cookies you can make, but if you don't care, they are also about the most heavenly morsels you ever tasted.

1½ cup graham cracker
  crumbs
1 can sweetened condensed
  milk
1 cup flaked coconut

1 cup (6 oz. package) semi-
  sweet chocolate
  morsels
½ cup chopped pecans (or
  walnuts)

Mix well and press into a well-greased 9" square pan. Bake at 350° about 30 minutes, until lightly browned around edges. Cut into small bars. (Makes 3 dozen 1½" squares)

INDEX